TALES FROM THE
RED & WHITES

TALES FROM THE
RED & WHITES

A collection of writing inspired
by Sunderland Association Football Club

Volume Two
Edited by Graeme Anderson, Lance Hardy
and Rob Mason

TALES FROM
www.talesfrom.com

First published in Great Britain in 2017
by Tales From

© 2017 The authors & Tales From Ltd

Printed and bound by Page Bros Ltd

Cover design by Steve Leard

ISBN 978-0-9932381-7-8

Tales From Ltd
107 Jupiter Drive, Hemel Hempstead, Herts HP2 5NU
Registered company number: 9082738

www.talesfrom.com
info@talesfrom.com

TALES FROM THE RED & WHITES

CONTENTS

THE EDITORS

GRAEME ANDERSON was the *Sunderland Echo*'s chief Sunderland AFC writer from 1996 to 2014, and he has written more words on the club than any other journalist in history. He was a contributor to *Tales from the Red and Whites, Volume One*, producing a chapter about the glory days of Niall Quinn and Kevin Phillips and co-writing Gary Rowell's story. In this volume, Graeme talks to Tony Coton, Stephen Elliott, Martin Scott and Stefan Schwarz.

LANCE HARDY is the author of *Stokoe, Sunderland and '73*, which was shortlisted for Football Book of the Year at the British Sports Book Awards and nominated for the British Society of Sports History Literary Prize. He was the editor of *Tales from the Red and Whites, Volume One*, also producing a chapter about the unbelievable and unjust 1976-77 season and co-writing Gary Bennett's story. In this volume Lance talks to Stan Anderson, Darren Holloway, John MacPhail and Tony Towers.

ROB MASON is Sunderland AFC club historian. He edited the Sunderland match programme and club magazine until 2017, having written for the programme since 1986. In total, he has written over 30 books on Sunderland. He was a contributor to *Tales from the Red and Whites, Volume One*, producing a chapter on the Team of All the Talents from the 1890s and co-writing Jim Montgomery's story. In this volume Rob talks to Gordon Armstrong, Shaun Elliott and Vic Halom.

INTRODUCTION

Welcome to the second volume of *Tales from the Red and Whites*. In this edition Graeme Anderson, Lance Hardy and Rob Mason have spent many months compiling and interviewing members of a Sunderland AFC XI that we hope has something for everyone.

The players in this book span a period of six decades: from the days of Len Shackleton to Roy Keane. There are many stories of promotions, relegations, cup runs, friendships, fall outs and much more. There is plenty in the following pages for Sunderland fans to reminisce about, but there is also a lot to learn as well, with more than a few exclusives along the way.

Our sincere thanks to all the contributors for taking the time to talk to us, and making this book so special.

We salute you all.

Up the Red and Whites!

1

Tony Coton played one more match for Sunderland than there are chapters in this book.

The story you are about to read starts at the end, with the final moment of a near 20-year playing career that commenced with a first-minute penalty save against Sunderland for Birmingham City.

Tony, a boyhood Blues fan, was a young lad at St Andrew's when Jim Montgomery was there as a veteran. He would play 615 fewer games for Sunderland than all-time appearance-maker Monty but had a top-class career concluding with the cameo for Sunderland that crashed in calamitous circumstances for keeper and club.

The other 10 players in volume two of *Tales from the Red and Whites* played over 2,000 games between them but Tony's tale illustrates that to have played even briefly for The Lads is something that can stay with you forever.

TONY COTON

'It's broke, it's broke!' winces Tony Coton, looking down at his right leg as his gloves dig deep into the firm turf of the Dell to steady himself against the pain.

It is 3.26 p.m. on 19 October 1996: the last minute of his playing career.

Nil-nil at Southampton and a sixth clean sheet out of 12 beckons for the Sunderland goalkeeper but that hardly matters now, as the injury is examined.

'It'll just be badly bruised,' says physio Nigel Carnell who has pulled the sock down, removed the shin pad and can see only a slight abrasion. 'It's broke,' replies Coton.

Many years later, as we sit having a coffee on the breezy terrace of Stockton's David Lloyd Tennis Centre, the former keeper explains, 'You know your own body and I knew it was broken, no matter how it looked, no matter what anyone said. It's not the broken one that gives me the issue these days, it's the left knee – wear and tear and nine operations on it. So I was no stranger to injury, it goes with the territory.'

Sunderland's eternal kit man John Cooke is delegated to accompany the distraught goalkeeper to hospital as Coton's initial state of shock gives way to waves of pain. As the stretcher reaches the tunnel, Coton moves his forearm to cover his face.

'Could be just bad bruising, TC,' offers Cooke, solemnly, as they leave the ground; oxygen and painkillers administered.

'It's broke,' says Coton, who also gives the same reply to the exact same optimistic diagnosis this time delivered by the ambulance medic.

At the hospital, the radiographer puts him in place for an X-ray and reassures Sunderland's number one that it looks just like bad bruising.

'It's broke.'

'Well, Tony, we'll see.'

Disappearing behind the protective screen, the radiographer examines the findings as Cooke peers over her shoulder.

'Oh,' she says. 'Actually, you're right, Tony. There *is* a break. It's your tibia. And . . . your fibula. Oh, and there's another one and another one. I've never seen as many breaks as this. Oh, and another one.'

'*Well, finally* . . . !' says the exasperated Coton, the relief at being believed temporarily blocking out for a moment both the pain and the implications.

Cookie the kit man's eyebrows mark the discovery of each break with a rise.

'By the end, they'd disappeared into his hairline,' recalled Coton with his trademark half-smile.

A thought occurs to the stricken shot-stopper: 'Hey, Cookie! What's the score?'

'We're losing, TC: 3-0 down, a couple of minutes left,' and on that news the keeper slumps wearily back onto his bed.

'Great.'

Shortly afterwards, in the post-match press conference at the Dell, I ask Peter Reid about the keeper's situation. 'Looks like tib and fib,' is the glum but matter-of-fact reply.

With that Coton all but disappears from public view for the rest of the season – the hospital bed and the treatment room are private places and he will spend a lot of time in both.

The football pitch, in contrast, is always in the spotlight, always the focus of fans' interest and, over the next six months, Wearside eyes would be glued to a story of so near but so far. Sunderland's solid start to the season will be built upon and in February they will be mid-table before the small squad is exhausted and a slide will accelerate towards an agonising last-day relegation at another southern venue – Wimbledon – despite the Black Cats having reached the supposed safety of the 40-points mark.

'It was a horrible day that,' says the keeper. 'We were poor. I think we were shot, really. But over the course of the whole season it had been some effort.'

Those six months from the Dell to the Dons are also a long road for Coton, though the journey begins with an element of farce as medics try and fail to shoehorn Coton's stretcher onto the football squad's small plane as it waits to leave the south coast.

After a few minutes of 'to you, to me' worthy of a *Monty Python* sketch, the undignified manoeuvring ends with him being returned to hospital before being flown to the north-east and another hospital the next day.

He will spend 10 days in a Teesside hospital – only a short distance from where we are now chatting – and he will have plenty of time to contemplate a shattering end, in every sense, to a season he felt was just gathering momentum for both himself and Sunderland.

The injury is also a body blow for Peter Reid, who has always appreciated it will take luck as well as judgement to keep the Black Cats in the top flight this season.

Reid is the reigning Manager of the Year after guiding, in the space of just 12 months, the relegation-threatened club he inherited to a first promotion to the Premier League.

But he knows it will represent just as big a success if he can somehow keep in the top flight the same basic squad that overachieved to win the First Division.

That summer, the Sunderland boss had very little money to strengthen, with money being diverted to a large extent towards the construction of a gleaming new stadium taking shape on the banks of the Wear.

Reid used the Sunderland board's money wisely with his two key signings: a striker and a keeper boasting vast experience of top-level football, his former players at Manchester City, Niall Quinn and Tony Coton. Coton would supplement the watertight back four on which promotion had been built; Quinn would provide the physical presence and ball retention up front which had previously been lacking.

Former Spurs and England player Paul Stewart was to bring even more Premier League experience, while Millwall's ferocious lion, Alex Rae, would add new energy and bite to central midfield.

They would all play their part but Reid felt that the pedigree of Coton, despite a lack of recent game time, would be vital.

'Reidy was big on a lot of things that served him well in those days: honest players, who were dedicated but could also have a laugh; players who would fit into a dressing room and bond it rather than unsettling it. He saw that in me, but he also knew that the likes of me and Quinny were used to playing at the highest level, and not only were we used to it but we'd done well there.

'Peter's concern was that he had some good players but the Premier League was unfamiliar to many of them, and he saw us as being there to help spread confidence and belief.

'That was particularly true of the defence, which he wanted to develop so that it was as good in the Premier League as it had been in the First Division. That was always going to be an interesting challenge in itself because, as I was to discover, Sunderland had two ball-playing centre-halves – Andy Melville and Richard Ord – playing in front of me!

'I'd had one ball-playing centre-half in front of me in my career but never two. Melville never panicked and was good on the ball, always composed, while Ordy couldn't make a clearance without a drag-back first or rolling his studs over it. It could give you heart failure at times!'

Coton arrived at Roker Park having proven himself one of the best keepers of his generation in an era with no shortage of fine goalkeepers. In the late eighties and early nineties Peter Shilton, Chris Woods, David Seaman and Dave Beasant were all selected ahead of him for England, but there were several spells over the year on Wearside where he could and should have made the cut. Like Sunderland great Jimmy Montgomery, he had inherited the mantle of 'best goalkeeper of his time not to earn a full England cap', regarded as the unluckiest of a group of keepers good enough to play for the Three Lions but who never did, Arsenal's John Lukic, Coventry's Steve Ogrizovic, Man United's Les Sealey included in their number.

He made an England 'B' team appearance in a 3-0 win over France in April 1992. But many Watford fans believe the reason he never won full honours was because he chose to stay loyal to the Hornets despite them being relegated from the top flight.

At Watford, Coton is a legend, quite literally – he became only the second player to be inducted into the Hornets' Hall of Fame, after Luther Blissett. And in his view he produced probably the best sustained keeping of his career during his time there, from 1984-90, earning three Player of the Season awards.

Born in the market town of Tamworth in the West Midlands, Coton was rejected at his boyhood club Wolves but made an instant impact at Birmingham City in 1977 when he (just) saved a penalty a mere 54 seconds into his debut. The penalty-taker? Sunderland's John Hawley.

Coton made more than 100 appearances for the Blues and almost 300 for Watford before moving to Man City in 1990, where his path was to cross those of Reid and Quinn.

His six seasons in the top flight at Maine Road, though they were to be interrupted by injuries and falling out of favour amid boardroom politics, still brought close to 200 appearances and two more Player of the Season awards. Reid saw Coton's qualities up close and coveted the keeper's signing soon after joining Sunderland. The England selectors might have underestimated Coton's qualities but the Black Cats' boss did not.

A man's man, the 6 foot 3 inch keeper dominated his penalty area as if his life depended on it. A talker, he commanded his defence too, constantly coaxing and cajoling them through the game and taking on the responsibility of ensuring the defence worked as a unit. He had all the attributes of a big keeper but he was also nimble and athletic; he was a brave shot-stopper but also possessed a sixth sense for danger and positioned himself accordingly.

As well as all that, he was a great character off the field whose sense of humour helped bond any dressing room.

Having decided to find a replacement for established Roker keeper Alec Chamberlain, Reid was encouraged by news that Coton was being frozen out at Maine Road after recovering from injury – chairman Francis Lee being keen on the purge of senior players, which he thought would refresh the club but eventually helped lead to its relegation.

Coton might have fancied an escape from languishing in City's reserves as the first team struggled but the first time the keeper heard of Sunderland's interest, and a surprise swap deal, he was having none of it!: 'I went into see manager Alan Ball because I wasn't playing and he said, "You've got no future here but Sunderland have come in for you, and I like their left-back Martin Scott, so we're looking to do a player-exchange."

'"I ain't going to Sunderland!" I said.

'I had nothing against Sunderland, mind you, but I was right in the middle of buying another house in Manchester, had proven myself at City, and leaving hadn't even crossed my mind. I've only gone to see about getting my first-team place back and out of the blue I'm suddenly told I'm moving to the far end of the country! I said I wasn't going and I left it at that.

'But I spoke to Peter to find out what was going on and he said he wanted me but he had no money and wasn't going to lose Scotty. He said that he would come back in for me in the summer when he might have a bit of money to spend.

'Sunderland were due to play Man United in the FA Cup a few days later so we agreed to meet up at Old Trafford to chat about it further.

'It turned out afterwards that he was chatting about his plans for me to Alex Ferguson and it was a lightbulb moment for Fergie, who rang me up on the way home and asked me to meet him. He was very frank with me and said, "Look, [I wasn't going to play at City, Sunderland couldn't afford me . . .] so why not try the experience of being at Man United?"

'It was a difficult one for me with Peter Schmeichel there, but the way he explained it was honest and brilliant. He said Peter was the best there was but that he'd noticed chinks in his armour – he was missing training, his performances were dropping – and he'd put it down to the fact that Peter wasn't being challenged enough. Fergie said, "Peter knows he's an automatic starter and that can affect you mentally, but I know he respects you for what you've done at Man City and if you come in you'll challenge him."

'Man United were trying to chase Newcastle down at the time, who were 12 points ahead at the top of the table, and Fergie said, "If you challenge Peter, he'll take his game to a whole new level and we need that. If it happens, if Peter gets back to his best, we'll catch Newcastle: they'll fold. Then, if you still want to go in the summer, I'll honour it."

Coton signed.

'It shows you just how smart he was as a manager,' he reflects. 'It was great training with Peter Schmeichel, and he was brilliant, as Fergie predicted he might be. He did take it to a new level, and nowhere more so than at St James' Park where Eric Cantona scored and United won 1-0.

'I was in the away dugout watching it all with all that noise and atmosphere and we should have lost by five or six that night but for Schmeichel.

'Later, after United had won the league and cup Double (beating Liverpool in the FA Cup final) we were having a celebration out when Fergie came over to me, put his hand on my shoulder and said, "Well, you might not have played, but you've done your job." And I appreciated that – he didn't have to say that.'

Ferguson wanted to keep Coton but the keeper was determined to leave – seeing all that first-team action, training with United's players, had whetted his appetite.

'I was in my mid-30s but I wasn't into comfort zones. I wanted to play first-team football in the time remaining to me.'

What he didn't know was which club to join.

'I had options but it came down to two – Wolves or Sunderland,' he reveals. 'Wolves seemed the right choice for numerous reasons: a lot of my family supported Wolves; the club was local to me; and it was also the club where I started, so it seemed fitting that I might end my career there. I met Mark McGhee and he offered me the same terms as Sunderland.'

But then there was Sunderland.

And Reidy.

'I talked it over with my family and then I picked up the phone to Mark McGhee to accept, and in the middle of the phone ringing, I changed my mind,' Coton recollects. '"Better the devil you . . ." I thought, and I knew Reidy. It just felt as though it would be familiar territory, linking up with Reidy and Quinny again and, at that stage of my career, I wanted that certainty.'

Coton's arrival on Wearside in July 1996 was treated by fans generally in a similar vein to that of Niall Quinn's signing: respect for his top-flight background but a player viewed as a steady rather than spectacular performer, someone not in the first-team frame elsewhere, being given a chance to revive his career on Wearside.

Reid, in contrast, had witnessed new his keeper's heroics many times down the years and, knowing what he was getting, was delighted at finally getting the £600,000 signing over the line.

The only issue was the 35-year-old's lack of competitive games.

He had kept four clean sheets in his last six first-team games for City, but that had been in the 1993-94 season and after that, he had been kept ticking over with training and reserve-team matches.

'I suffered a blood clot in my thigh which kept me out for seven months,' explains Coton. 'And then when I got back I was fighting to regain my place, plus, as everyone I think knows, there was a lot of politics going on at Man City at the time.'

Coton had been fit for a while at Man City and had been training and continued to play reserve games at Man United, but he needed competitive matches and got stuck into Sunderland's pre-season tour across the Irish Sea that summer.

'We never conceded in the four games we played in Ireland and I was happy about that, but in Richard Ord's testimonial against Steaua Bucharest we lost 1-0, so that kept me on my toes going into the season.'

The start of the campaign couldn't have gone much better for Coton, with his debut producing a goalless draw against fellow promotion side Leicester City at Roker Park.

It was a game of few chances but, in the 65th minute, the new keeper played his part when a poor back pass from Paul Bracewell was intercepted by Emile Heskey and Coton made an important one-on-one block.

In the following game, a 4-1 win at Nottingham Forest in which Quinn scored twice, the keeper was delighted with the discipline of the defence in front of him. And then in the away trip to Anfield Coton made his mark again in a goalless draw, by producing vital saves to deny Robbie Fowler and Stan Collymore.

Coton had passed a late fitness test for that game, overcoming an Achilles injury which left him unable to take his side's goal-kicks, but of more importance to him was the 2-1 defeat at Roker Park to Newcastle United which left him feeling he might have done better in that match.

'That was a turning point for me,' he admits. 'I'd done well enough but I hadn't played much first-team football, and we so wanted to do well against Newcastle. The problem for me was that because I was very much a veteran at that stage, I had arrived as a goalkeeping coach and I felt I had to take the role seriously. So I was organising and holding training sessions for our other keepers – David Preece, Phil Naisbett and Chris Porter – as well as trying to fit in my own training.

'After the Newcastle game I had words with the management and said that while I would still do goalkeeping coaching when I could – like during international breaks, for example – from then on I had to put myself, and the first team, first.

'I immediately felt better about things, much more relaxed, and in the next game against Derby County, even though we lost, I felt much better in terms of my energy and concentration levels.

'It was a tough game to lose though. Dickie Ord got sent off before the half-hour mark at the Baseball Ground and we were up against it.'

Coton made numerous saves – stopping a free-kick, a long-range piledriver, a point-bank block, a lob tipped over – and was only beaten from the penalty spot after the clumsiest of challenges by Gareth Hall.

'Even though we lost, I felt I'd done well,' said Coton. 'I was starting to find my best form again.'

Writing in the *Football Echo*, my colleague Geoff Storey agreed: 'Coton produced his best display of the season to keep Sunderland in the hunt,' he noted.

The next league game brought a clean sheet for Coton and a goal for Steve Agnew against Coventry City as Sunderland gained their first home win of the season.

The keeper turned a Gary McAllister shot spectacularly over the bar, denied Dion Dublin from a close-range header and, in the closing stages, pushed a Noel Whelan effort around the post.

Clean sheets in both legs of a Second Round League Cup tie against former club Watford boosted confidence further before a fine individual display ended in inevitable defeat to Arsenal at Highbury after Sunderland were reduced to nine men following the first-half dismissals of Martin Scott and Paul Stewart.

'That was some game,' smiles Coton. 'Man United and Arsenal were the top two teams in the country and that day Arsenal had players like Paul Merson, David Platt, Patrick Vieira and Ian Wright playing for them, so it was always going to be difficult with 11 men, never mind nine!'

Sunderland had actually had the better of the game until Scott's sending off in the 21st minute for his second bookable offence. When Stewart followed him down the tunnel in the 39th minute, having handled the ball in two separate incidents, Sunderland's hopes were more about avoiding a rout rather than avoiding a defeat.

'Reidy brought Darius Kubicki on after Scotty was sent off so that we'd have an established back four, and then it was just backs to the wall after that. There were times I was looking to clear the ball upfield but there were none of our players even in their half!'

Sunderland hung on until the 73rd minute when John Hartson bundled home, but the reason Reid's men conceded a second just before full-time was because they were chasing an equaliser!

'We took heart from that match because the scoreline could have been much, much worse,' says Coton. 'We were at the home of one of the two best teams in the land and down to nine men but we'd restricted them, showed how much spirit and organisation we had and avoided a drubbing.'

One more game – a derby boost with a 2-2 draw against a star-studded Boro side – followed before that day of hell at the Dell.

Coton kept six clean sheets in the 11 full games he played and his loss, along with serious injuries to Martin Scott and Niall Quinn in the previous weeks were losses which Reid's small squad struggled to overcome for the remainder of the season.

Coton, meanwhile, was facing the agony of long-distance recuperation, knowing he had the rest of the season on the sidelines – and the likelihood that his career was over.

'I was in the hospital in Teesside for 10 days, waiting for the swelling to go down before they put the plaster on,' he remembers. 'After six weeks, it still hadn't healed. I had a big cricket ball-sized lump on my shin. They tried experimental surgery hoping it would heal but it didn't, and I wasted more or less a year hoping that that would work.

'Then they put a rod down the shin and removed the bone callus, but three surgeons said, "You'll really struggle to get back from this" – and when I couldn't kneel down after the rod was put in, I knew I had no chance.'

Coton had had no clear view of what he might do next but jumped at an offer to coach Sunderland reserves the following season, and he led the second string to the league title in the same season Sunderland reached the play-off final at Wembley.

But when a reshuffle took place, with Coton to be offered a position of less pay and responsibility, he opted to activate a clause in his contract giving him access to an insurance payment for the premature end of his career.

That was when the bombshell was dropped on him that the club had not paid the insurance policy because the premiums had been deemed too high, given Coton's age.

'They were trying to wing it and it backfired,' says Coton.

At a meeting with club chairman Bob Murray in the boardroom, Coton was told morally and legally he didn't have a leg to stand on – an ironic turn of phrase, given the state of Coton's legs.

'I said, "No, morally and legally, you're wrong,"' recalls the keeper.

Coton won his case – the club settling out of court just as the case was about to be heard. But in the process he lost his job – the then Sunderland club secretary Mark Blackbourne putting him on gardening leave via fax before his eventual departure.

'Blackbourne's fax asking me not to come to take control of a reserve game was the beginning of the end,' says Coton. 'It was sad that it ended that way because I really enjoyed my time at Sunderland. These things happen, though – the club messed up – and I had to do what was right for me and my family. Sadly that meant I was out of work at the end of it.'

Not for long, though.

Shortly afterwards, Coton was taken on as goalkeeping coach by Ferguson, now Sir Alex, at Man United. The Red Devils' boss was fully aware of what the former keeper could bring to the party, and over the next spectacular decade of success, from 1997–2007, Coton had a front-row seat at the Theatre of Dreams. It only ended when that troublesome left knee crumpled underneath him in the very last kick of a goalkeeping session and he was no longer able to take coaching.

'Surgeons said that my knee was like papier mâché and if I continued coaching I would end up in a wheelchair. So that was that,' he says, injury having ended his job in football for a second time.

'What an experience it was, though, to have been at Man United during those years. I missed playing football an awful lot when I had to give it up but coaching at Sunderland helped me get over it. I threw myself into it and David Kelly says that to this day I'm the only person he's seen carrying out a coaching session leaning on a crutch with his leg in plaster!

'You always miss playing but getting into coaching and being part of the set-up at Man United was a great opportunity to be part of an amazing era.'

Coton regrets now that he didn't take up offers of other posts at Old Trafford when his goalkeeping coaching career came to an end: 'I was all over the place mentally when I got the news on my knee and decided I just wanted a complete break rather than taking up some other post.'

But he remained in the game and, many years on, has enjoyed the role of Director of Recruitment (the old chief scout job) at Aston Villa, where he works closely with former Sunderland manager Steve Bruce.

We hold our interview for this book in the tennis club in Stockton because he has brought his middle daughter, 23-year-old Beth, up for professional tennis coaching exams – sporting ability runs in the family.

His youngest daughter Chloe, 19, was born at Teesside Hospital just a couple of miles up the road, during his stay with the Black Cats, and he remains fond of his time at the club despite the injury, despite the end of his career and despite the litigation.

'They were a really good bunch of lads and we used to have such a good laugh,' he says. 'The team spirit was fantastic and yet the person who was often on the receiving end of the humour during my time there was Kevin Ball – who pretty much ran the club – and his chief tormentor was Paul Stewart. When Paul and me and Quinny arrived together we were senior pros and were amazed at how strictly Bally ran it. "Is he always like this?" we asked when he used to take great pleasure in pinning up the dress code ahead of matches and barking out his orders. One of the best captains you'll ever find, Bally, but he ran Sunderland Football Club with an iron fist. It was his rules, no other rules, and he was good at it. He liked it. And it's great to have a captain who will do everything off the pitch as well as on it.

'But I'd known Paul Stewart from England squads and it was a red rag to a bull to him – Bally will tell you we had his life, and so will other people around the club. With Stewy, if he ever felt a twinge in a muscle or an ache in his back, I'd tell him it was Bally sticking pins in his Paul Stewart voodoo doll!

'Bally loved giving out the dress-code rules: he would take great pride, Friday, pinning the sheet up, telling us what time to be on the bus, what to wear to travel, what to wear for the game: black polo shirt, red tracksuit to travel; white polo shirt, black tracksuit for the game.

'But one game when he went out of the room, we said we'd do it in reverse, the exact opposite. Reidy knew what we were up to but he loved it – team spirit and all that – so Bally gets on the bus and you could see he couldn't work it out. He's looking around and we're saying nothing and you could see his mind's whirring because he's now dressed in exactly the opposite of what we are.

'Then Stewy says, "That's a fine that, Bally."

'The young lads were loving it: Bally's leadership – or dictatorship – they'd had it so long that they just loved it.

'Bally couldn't handle it, he got his Filofax out and he checked that, and then when we still didn't believe him, he got off the bus, retrieved his original notice and was waving it around in our faces, saying, "See! SEE?!"

'Players had tears running down their faces.

'We had him on toast and he hated Paul Stewart with a passion. Bally said he drove him to the brink – he was like Blakey in *On the Buses* – and Paul used to be driving into work in the morning going, "Oh, TC I've got a great one for him."'

The skipper was not one to be messed with though, as the keeper recalls from a now infamous fancy-dress Christmas party held by Sunderland players in the city centre.

'It was something me and Quinny used to do at Man City and it always went down fantastically well, so we wanted to do it at Sunderland too,' remembers the keeper.

It was quite a roll call: Niall Quinn turning up as a monk; Coton with his broken leg appearing as a pirate – Long John Silver, of course; Mickey Gray and reserve-team player David Mawson, ringers for Starsky and Hutch; and there were also the Three Musketeers and Madonna.

'It was a long night and it had all gone well and I remember looking out of a window with one eye and seeing this nurse braying seven bells out of a bloke in the back alley. I nudged Quinny and said, "She's tough!" And then I said, "Bloody hell, it's Bally!" Turns out it was another group of lads out on their Christmas party and it had all got a bit narky, but they messed with the wrong guy in picking on Bally. There were loads of them, and we piled out to peace-keep, but then fists were flying and all of a sudden we were a part of it. This geezer took a swing at me so I jabbed him and he went back. I smashed him with my crutch and as I'd gone back to swing again I found myself in a bear hug from behind, lifted up and turned around the corner. It was Sam Allardyce, who had been brought in by Reidy as a coach at the time, saying, "Don't be stupid, man, you've got a broken bloody leg!"

'He often reminds me of that when I see him.'

The good times helped ease the disappointment of not being able to fulfil the mission he'd been brought into Sunderland to accomplish.

'I do regret that I never got to play at the Stadium of Light,' he says. 'I used to drive past it and watch it going up and look forward to what it would be like playing there. I wanted to be part of the transition. It would have been nice had it turned out differently, but I've no regrets, I've had a great career in football.'

Would it all have turned out differently had Coton stayed fit? We'll never know. And his replacement, Lionel Pérez, went on to establish himself as a fans' favourite with a regular string of spectacular saves.

But a few years ago, Reid said at a talk-in, 'If Quinny and TC had stayed fit that season, I think we would have stayed up,' before adding, 'Actually, if TC had stayed fit, I think we would have stayed up!'

It was quite a statement.

'He said that, did he?' muses Coton. 'Well, that's a nice thing for him to say. It would have been nice to find out! I was good at organising a back four, steadying a defence, giving it confidence. Kevin Ball used to say to me that just when he expected the ball to go in, I seemed to be in the right place. I'd got better and better at positioning myself and "sensing" a game and I think that's what Bally was on about. Who knows what would have happened. I felt I was just settling in and it was coming good.

'A lot of responsibility now rested on Lionel and my worry was that he always came out feet first at every opportunity, body splayed to dive at an attacker's feet – he was the only keeper I knew who wore a box because the ball kept hitting him there that often!

'It looked great and the fans loved it, but too often to my mind he'd block the ball but it would bounce off him and be put away, when he might have been better off standing up and using his balance and reach.

'Sometimes the best keepers don't have to make the spectacular saves others need to – if you organise your defence and do everything else right, you're protected, and then those special saves come only as a last resort. I tried to coach it out of Lionel but he wasn't having it. My fear was it would cost us long-term and him too.

'And then, of course, the play-off final came and at the end of it Reidy and I were walking off the pitch and he said, "You've told me all season it might cost me, and it just has: go and get me another keeper.

'So I did.'

That keeper was Thomas Sørensen, a keeper who served Sunderland wonderfully well from 1998–2003. But his signing, a matter of historical fact now, was a damn close run thing at the time.

Andy King, then chief scout, asked Coton to take a look at this young keeper who played for Odense in Denmark and was reported to be quite something.

'I went out to watch a game but as it turned out it was a reserve game – literally one up from a parks pitch: no stands, railings around the outside, a running track.

'I stood by the goal and I thought physically, yes, he made one or two good saves, he talked to his teammates, and I came back saying, yes, he was well worth another follow-up.

'But then we got wind that Schmeichel had him earmarked for Man United and an approach was being planned. It was now or never because we felt as soon as Tommy heard of Peter and United's interest, he would sign for them. I was put on the spot by the club and they asked me if I was sure that this was our fella – after one reserve game! It was a massive call.

'But I put my name to it. He was a bit rough around the edges but we could work on that, and I just thought the lad has so much potential – you could see he had that smart, focused Scandinavian mentality – and we didn't want to take the risk of missing out on him.'

Sørensen went on to play almost 200 games for Sunderland during their Premier League glory years under Reid, playing an important role in the Black Cats' top-flight success. The Dane played more than 100 times for his country and spent nearly 20 years in the top flight. Coton reflects, 'If I didn't do what I wanted to do for Sunderland on the pitch, I feel as though I did all right for them off it – Thomas Sørensen was not a bad gift to leave the club.'

That's typical Coton: the naturally optimistic approach to life, the desire to look for humour in any given situation, which has stood him in good stead and allowed him to cope with whatever life has thrown at him, including successfully surviving a heart condition.

We've enjoyed our talk and reminiscing about the old days, sitting outside the tennis centre with my old *Football Echo*'s spread out across the table as a mental prompt for him.

As I pack up, we begin to chat about the huge but unintended effect one man had on Sunderland's season: Southampton's bustling forward Egil Østenstad.

It was Østenstad who put Coton out of the game in the two team's first encounter of the season, and then scored the only goal of the game in a vital late-season match at Roker Park which would have made Sunderland safe had they won it.

'Never heard from him, not in the past 20 years,' discloses Coton. 'Never really thought about it, though, just like I've never looked for footage of the incident. Never seen it.

'Anyway, there's no blame attached to him, it was a nothing thing. Matt Le Tissier swung one in, I came out for it and he slid in – that's football.'

Then he spots a quote from the Norwegian in the *Football Echo* the week after the injury: 'We both went for the ball,' says the striker. 'I heard the crack and at first I thought it was my leg

that was broken – it really hurt. Then he said, "My leg's broken."
I know what it's like to break my leg, I've done it twice, but I
came back and I am sure he can.'

All these years later the quote seems to satisfy the grizzled
keeper. 'Fair enough,' he nods.

And then, just as I'm packing away, a gust of wind springs
up to blow copies of my beloved *Football Echo* off the table.
I turn quickly to see Coton having instinctively grabbed the
papers, his arms spread wide, a clump of them in either hand.

'Look,' he says with a half-smile. 'Another clean sheet.'

2

Having come through the youth system as a local lad, **Darren Holloway** was a teak-tough defender in the early years at the Stadium of Light, but one who sooner rather than later suffered more than his fair share of injuries.

Here he talks about the changing face of football during his playing career, his debt to Red and White legend Pop Robson, his sudden exit from Sunderland and his recent introduction to management as Alun Armstrong's assistant at National League North side Blyth Spartans.

There is also the small matter of a famous match under the twin towers at Wembley against Charlton Athletic in 1998 . . .

DARREN HOLLOWAY

MEETS LANCE HARDY

It is likely that many if not all of the Sunderland players who were cruelly beaten in the First Division play-off final by Charlton Athletic at Wembley Stadium in 1998 would have had personal regrets on the night of that agonising Spring Bank Holiday Monday.

Kevin Phillips, with a post-Second World War club record of 35 goals to his name that season, would no doubt have despaired at the injury that took him out of the match with less than 20 minutes of normal time remaining with Sunderland leading 3-2; substitute Daniele Dichio may have replayed his missed volley from a few yards out that would surely have wrapped up the contest shortly afterwards; goalkeeper Lionel Pérez might still ask himself why he came running off his line to palm away an 85th-minute corner, which resulted in Richard Rufus heading into an empty net to force extra time; and, of course, Michael Gray would rue his crucial missed penalty for a long time to come. Sunderland lost 7-6 on spot kicks after a 4-4 draw. It was an exhilarating and exhausting contest that had a feeling of complete emptiness at the end of it.

Darren Holloway was Sunderland's 20-year-old right-back that day. His own personal regret happened before the match had even kicked off and, indirectly, it could have impacted on the way the day went, including the heart-stopping final scenario of the penalty shoot-out.

Nearly 20 years on, the two of us are sitting together in a Durham hotel, close to the former player's home town of Crook, having a drink and reminiscing about his time at Sunderland and the biggest match he ever played in his career.

'The one really big regret I have about the play-off final is that I never warmed up properly,' Darren remembers. 'It was my first time at Wembley and I was struggling with my back. I had an issue with it prior to the play-off semi-finals against Sheffield United and I didn't know what it was about. It was stiffening up and causing me pain. There was a Sunderland mascot on his lonesome at Wembley and I ended up kicking the ball around with him while the rest of the lads were doing a proper warm-up. Looking back, it was obviously the wrong thing to do. I should have done a proper warm-up. But I just thought there was a young lad here, probably six or seven, he's come down for his big day, and he looks lost. So I ended up having a tap about with him.

'I didn't start the game well, probably as a result of that,' Darren adds. 'I got booked pretty early on and then I got subbed at half-time. I think it was a good decision to take me off, actually. After getting booked, I was on tenterhooks. I had quite a quick winger in Neil Heaney on my side of the pitch, and I would have been worried that I would get sent off anyway – there was always that chance.

'Another regret – and nobody knows this – is that I was one of the five down to take a penalty!

'We practised penalties,' Darren adds. 'We got asked who wanted to take one and I said, "OK." So, I was down to be a penalty-taker. But, of course, I never got that opportunity. Then, obviously, it all comes down to Mickey and I think he felt the whole of Sunderland on his shoulders and ended up probably doing the worst penalty I have seen in my life. Mickey had a good left foot. It was just the pressure scenario and it obviously got to him. I didn't think he wanted to take one. He wasn't too keen. It just got further down the line where someone needed to take one. He was the seventh. It is hard to put it into words. I remember Reidy telling us to take in the moment, and looking back I probably never did. I was disappointed with my own performance, but it was obviously very disappointing for us all. I really wanted us to get promoted and I felt I had not done myself justice.

'For a good few days afterwards I was in a bad place,' Darren says. 'I dare say a lot of us were. We weren't our usual selves. Some took longer than others to get over it. The timing of it didn't help as we were on our holidays! I felt sorry for myself and I just wanted to stew for a good few days. It did hit me hard. We never spoke about it much as a group but I can guarantee that there would have been a lot of lads in the same situation as I was in.'

Despite that heartbreaking final chapter at Wembley, the 1997-98 campaign was one of the most exciting seasons in Sunderland's recent history. The club moved into the Stadium of Light, welcomed and motivated by the haunting music of Sergei Prokofiev and home crowds of over 40,000 fans as Peter Reid assembled one of the youngest defences in the league to go alongside some supreme attacking talent. They stylishly accumulated 90 points during the regular season. Somehow, it wasn't quite enough to win automatic promotion.

However, after 10 league matches, Sunderland had only 13 points on the board. Furthermore, a 4-0 defeat at Reading in October was accompanied by vitriol from the visiting supporters as the players and staff returned to the team coach. In hindsight, this was to be a significant turning point in the Peter Reid era. Within a couple of weeks, Sunderland had an entirely new back four: Kevin Ball was moved from central defence into midfield, and Andy Melville, Chris Makin, and Martin Scott were dropped; Jody Craddock and Darren Williams formed a new central defensive partnership, Michael Gray was moved from left midfield to left-back, and Darren Holloway was brought in at right-back. These four players – with an average age of 21 – were to be the backbone of the team for the rest of the season.

'I was in the stand at Reading and we were really poor,' Darren recalls. 'I thought to myself, "If I don't get in now, then I will probably never get in." This was my moment. I was still relatively young, but the gaffer [Peter Reid] and Sacko [Bobby Saxton] would have me travelling to away games with the first team, whether that was for my experience or to get me used to the environment, I don't know. I was doing well in the reserves so I think it was done to make me feel a part of it. They would tell me to go and get changed, do the warm-up and then come back and sit and watch the game. I had been travelling with the squad for quite a long time, staying overnight in the hotels, spoiling myself by getting steak – as you could in those days before the pasta police came in – and just feeling part of it.'

The man who had the biggest influence in Holloway's development at Sunderland was a former Roker Park legend, who had scored 68 goals during three different spells at the club and was now running the reserve team – with Holloway as a centre-half and captain – for Reid.

'I have to thank Pop Robson more than anybody for getting me in the Sunderland side,' Darren says. 'I joined as a centre-half. I had played in the centre of midfield, but I think they saw me more defensively, and in those days your two central midfielders were box-to-box midfielders – you never had holding midfielders when I was playing youth-team football.

So I ended up playing centre-half, which I enjoyed. I liked the one-v-one competitive nature with the centre-forward, and I wasn't afraid to get it down and play. Pop came up to me in the reserves one day and said, "Do you think you could play right-back? Because, if so, I think you can get into the first team." At the time, Gareth Hall was playing right-back [1996-97], but Pop thought I could do a better job. Now, bearing in mind I had not played full-back since I was about 10-years-old in district football, it was kind of alien to me, but I put my trust in him and I said I would give it a go. As it turned out, it got me into the side.

'You see a lot of centre-halves do it in modern day football: John O'Shea, Wes Brown and Chris Smalling all did it at Manchester United. I didn't think I would continue as a right-back, but it was the chance I needed to get into the first team. So, it was a case of me learning my trade in that position and Pop gave me that opportunity.

'I had known Pop from the time I was at the Manchester United School of Excellence as a boy and he was a coach there,' Darren adds. 'When I was released at the age of 15, he advised my dad to take me to York City, because it had a really good youth set-up. While I was there, Jim Morrow, who worked with the youth team at Sunderland, showed an interest in me. I went up to train at Sunderland and they wanted me. I now had a choice between being a big fish in a little pond or a little fish in a big pond. It was the size of Sunderland – and the fact it was local to me – that made my mind up to go there.

'Terry Butcher was the manager at the time and I have still got the newspaper clipping of me signing my forms at Roker Park. I went with my mam to Foster's in Bishop Auckland and we bought a black and white dogtooth blazer. It was probably a bit too big for me, but I thought it looked really smart. When I turned up at Sunderland, Terry Butcher had the same jacket on!

'In all truth, the youth set-up at Sunderland in those days was poor,' Darren admits. 'I was 15-and-a-half and I was playing with the Under-19s. I would love to tell you that I was a brilliant player at that age but I think the fact of the matter is that they weren't as strong as they probably should have been for the size of the club that they were. This meant that I ended up playing with lads that were a lot older than me. I was competitive and I was always able to tackle and stuff so I quite enjoyed the challenge, but looking back it probably says a lot about the deficiencies of the club at that time rather than me being particularly spectacular.

'My first-year YTS [1994-95] was done with Jim Montgomery and George Herd, who were old school but they were brilliant as well, and I enjoyed it. Whatever they said went. I think there was something in my background that enabled me to take it all on board and roll with it. You had to do what they wanted you to do to get on.

'When Peter Reid came in he changed the backroom staff and that meant that Jim and George left. It had been a difficult time for the club when I was a YTS. There wasn't a good vibe about the place and I remember fans demonstrating outside Roker Park and calling for Bob Murray's head. The first team had a really bad spell under Mick Buxton and they just couldn't win at home. Nobody likes to see people lose their jobs, but the decision to sack Mick and his assistant Trevor Hartley and get Reidy in was the right one. A change had to happen and it happened for the best.

'So, the youth team I ended up playing with included the likes of Michael Bridges, who obviously did really well, Sam Aiston, who went on to make a career for himself, and Paul

Heckingbottom, who is now the manager at Barnsley. It was now a totally different story and, in all honesty, that had a lot to do with the people that Peter Reid brought in, such as Pop Robson. He also had Bobby Saxton, Ricky Sbragia and Paul Bracewell, although he didn't really get involved in the coaching side because he was still playing at that time.

'For me, Pop was the standout coach,' Darren adds. 'He would keep me back in training so that he could help my development. I never felt it was a hardship to do that because I knew it was going to benefit me. I always thought it was going to help me get to where I wanted to be. He had a lot of faith in me. He would knock on Reidy's door and say that I should be in the first team.

'By 19 I was captain of the reserves, which was a big thing because there were lads there who had played 300 league games and stuff like that, but Pop gave me that responsibility and I think that helped me grow. I had to act like a captain and organise people around the pitch. I got my first professional contract at 17 and I was over the moon with that. I still did my full YTS because they still made me do all my jobs and all that but I was now on four times more money than the other lads who were on the YTS with me. In truth, I was probably playing for peanuts by the time that I got into the first team, but I was a council-estate lad who was now earning more than my dad had ever made, so I was happy. I wasn't chasing the money, I was chasing the dream of being a professional footballer.

'Reidy saved the club from relegation, which was a big relief. He then took us up into the Premier League, but we came back down again the following season, and the timing of relegation ahead of our move into the new stadium was a big kick in the balls for us. But I think the fans saw what we were trying to do as a club and what we were trying to do in terms of playing football and they got behind us. We had a lovely new ground, a new team that was showing real ambition and trying to play decent football and everybody bought into it.'

Holloway was in the first-team squad for the 1997-98 campaign. He was still only 19 when the Stadium of Light era kicked off with a 3-1 win over Manchester City in front of a crowd of 38,827.

'I went out on loan to Carlisle United,' Darren says. 'I felt I had to do that to prove to Reidy that I was ready for first-team football. I think that helped me as well because Carlisle wanted to buy me and it got knocked back by Sunderland. After that, everything just fell into place for me. Obviously, it was the 4-0 defeat at Reading that got into Reidy's head that he had to change things around. As bad as that result was, it definitely gave me the chance that I needed.

'I made my debut at Stoke and I think the gaffer was cute in that sense because he knew it was an away game so it was less pressure on a young lad. I never looked back after that. It never fazed me. I enjoyed it and I gave it my all. After my debut, my focus was to make sure that I was in the team for the next one.

'It was a brilliant time. I always call it "a crest of a wave". We had a young back four in me, Jody Craddock, Daz Williams and Mickey Gray; the likes of Kevin Ball, Lee Clark and Alex Rae in midfield; a poor man's Beckham – as I used to call him – in Nicky Summerbee on the right-hand side, who had a great right foot and a brilliant delivery; on the other side we had someone who was totally different in Allan Johnston, who had a telepathic communication with Mickey on the left; add Niall Quinn and Kevin Phillips to that mix and we had a very good side.

'That season was so intense. People often ask me where the best stadium I ever played at was. I always say it was the Stadium of Light! I played at Anfield, Old Trafford and Wembley, but the Stadium of Light was the best. It was a brand new stadium and the atmosphere was electric. There was nothing like it. I have never been at an away game where I have felt that much noise and that much intensity as I did when playing at home that season. It was now a proper football club. From what I can remember of being a YTS and having to fight for jumpers in the laundry room when it was snowing outside, to go on to something like that in just a few years was incredible.

'Jody Craddock would always go in early to do a bit of stretching. He was probably beyond his years in that regard, and so he would be in the gym while some of us would still be in bed! We would get in, get changed, go outdoors, warm up, do the session that Reidy and Sacko put on, have a bit of bait and then shoot off home, relax, and do the same again the next day. It was basically living the dream – doing what I had always dreamt of doing.

'Training for me was massive. I got a nickname when I was staying in the hostel on the seafront and someone had Vinnie Jones's *Soccer's Hard Men* on video with Ron "Chopper" Harris on it. I got called "Chopper" Holloway and the nickname stuck – out of the digs and into the first team. But that was me: I was competitive in training because that is how I perceived I was going to play on a Saturday. I couldn't hold anything back. That, in essence, was the beauty of what Reidy had with us. How hard we worked in training probably goes under the radar a bit, but we used to train really hard together as a group. There was a terrific team spirit.'

So, what are Holloway's personal standout moments from a season that lives long in the memory of many Sunderland fans?

'The 3-0 win at Nottingham Forest is a good memory,' Darren reflects. 'We played very well that night and, to be honest, I always thought that we were better than Forest! Middlesbrough had some good players, so I thought they would go up, but I think we had a better team than Forest. I suppose we dropped points where we shouldn't have, and in the end we lost out to them.

'The Stoke game was special for me because it was my debut. I got man of the match against Charlton at The Valley and my mam has still got the bottle of champagne, which Reidy collected for me because I think he didn't want me in front of the cameras with it! We played Bradford City over the festive period in front of 40,000 and the atmosphere was brilliant, and the Sheffield United play-off match was also fantastic. We then had to set our minds on the play-off final.

'Wembley was a rollercoaster! It was up and down and up and down all the way. I soaked Reidy at one time after we scored a goal. I had a water bottle and I squirted it up in the air and it went all over the gaffer! People say that as a spectacle it was a great match, but being on the receiving end of something like that is certainly not great. It kicked a lot of our heads in. Even now, I think, "Lionel, don't come for it," whenever I see their third goal. But it's all ifs, buts and maybes now . . .

'At the end of the day, the lads bounced back the following season,' Darren says. 'We won the title with a record 105 points. So, the whole experience made us tighter as a group and more determined, simply because we didn't want to go down that path again. We were strong at managing ourselves and that helped us to recover from the heartache and do so well the following season. We would tell each other how it was. There were some strong characters in there. I was still relatively young myself but I would always stand my ground and speak up for myself if I thought I was right. It was something that I did naturally.

'But I was struggling with my back and it took me something in the region of five or six months to recover. I couldn't fathom out what was wrong. I must have seen about five different specialists, including one in Harley Street. In the end I was sent to Lilleshall, and within a week constant manipulation of my back freed it up. It was now a case of doing a rehab programme and getting fit again, but it took an awful long time and, unfortunately for me, that gave Chris Makin an opportunity to come back into the side and he did really well. So the timing of it wasn't great for me. If I had cemented my place, I think I could have kicked on and done really well. But it took me six months before I could even kick a ball again. So, even though I was a part of it all the following season, I didn't see myself as being a part of it. Yes, I got a league championship medal but I don't value it as highly as I probably should because I only made the odd appearance. When footballers get injured they can get depressed. Frustration is a light way of putting it.'

'When a team is doing well it is also very hard to knock on the manager's door,' Darren adds. 'But it never crossed my mind to be anywhere else. This was my club and I wanted to get established in any position that I could to get into the team.

'We had a very good squad and we were adding quality to it with Don Hutchison, who was a good footballer; my good mate, Gavin McCann, who played for England; and also Stefan Schwarz, who played for Fiorentina and in World Cups for Sweden. Reidy was bringing in players like that and the club was on the ladder to getting further up the Premier League. Obviously, I wanted to be a part of it. If you're happy on the bench then there is something wrong with you in my opinion.'

It would be March 2000 before Holloway was to make his first Premier League start, at Leicester in a 5-2 defeat.

'We got run ragged that day,' Darren recalls. 'But it gave me a taste of what it was all about. I never thought that the Premier League was above me. I always wanted to better myself and my whole time at Sunderland was always about me striving to do that. I am a proud person and if I didn't do well in training it would prey on my mind. I always wanted to be the best, even if I couldn't be the best. That is how I approached every training session. My desire was basically the main drive that got me to where I was as a professional.'

Sunderland finished the 1999-2000 season in seventh place in the top flight – their highest league finish since 1954-55 – with Kevin Phillips winning the European Golden Shoe with 30 Premier League goals. The good times were definitely back on Wearside.

'Everything was changing so quickly in football at that time,' Darren says. 'We now had sports science and the training methods were also different, so it was no longer "Bobby Saxton's run round six goals, come back in and we'll have a game of football". That was long gone! It was now much more technical. Our diet changed and we were staying behind to eat pasta, chicken, vegetables and fruit in the canteen together rather than jumping in our cars and driving off after training. Everything was planned and organised to give us the best opportunity to perform.

'The social aspect of it started to be different as well. The gaffer used to have us going away for weekends. It was classed as training but we never took any boots, just our dancing gear! It helped us in terms of team spirit. Most of us were British lads and we socialised together. The foreign players didn't socialise as much and so that began to change how Reidy did his bonding sessions. Everything became a lot more serious around this time. Arsène Wenger made the point about not putting diesel in a Formula One car, and it makes sense. But that was the environment I had been brought up in. People talk about a drinking culture and, yes, if we had an opportunity to go out and have a drink, we would, but that all changed drastically and more emphasis was now put on us as individuals. I would like to say that it didn't affect how Reidy managed things, but it probably did in a sense because that is what he was used to as well and so that is what he used to build the strong team spirit that we had. It was professional to an extent, but everything was now becoming very different. We had to be at a certain level of fitness on a Saturday to play against professional athletes, because that is what footballers became.

'When I first started playing we would go to places and you could guarantee that we would bump into players from other teams having a drink. It was a level playing field, but it all changed due to the foreign influence. I liked a night out on a Saturday after a game or possibly a drink with my mates back in Crook on a Sunday afternoon. But I turned down a lot of nights out. I just couldn't afford to do it. You can't party when you have a game coming up, particularly at the top level.

'It boils down to dedication, and it is beneficial. But if you asked me if I would enjoy it as much today as I did back then? Probably not, if I am honest. I think a lot of the players who were with me at Sunderland would say the same. The football was great and socially it was really good as well. That was due to the team spirit. It went hand in hand, on and off the pitch.'

Back to fitness, Holloway returned to the first team and was given a man-marking job on Nwankwo Kanu on the opening day of the 2000-01 season as Sunderland beat Arsenal 1-0 at the Stadium of Light.

'It was only at Sunderland that I was given man-marking roles,' Darren says. 'One was Joe Cole, when he was at West Ham; one was Paul Scholes at Old Trafford; and the other one was Kanu. From what I remember, we just bullied them. I stayed close to him throughout the game and he didn't appreciate that. My role was to try and stifle him, stop him from getting on the ball and creating something. I didn't get massively involved with having the ball, I was just conscious of where he was. It was a great result for us to turn them over at the start of the season. They were brilliant footballers – a better team than us by far – but we got the result.'

The future seemed to be bright again for the young defender. Holloway kept his place in the Sunderland side for the first five games of the season. Then came a bombshell . . .

'To this day, I have no idea why I had to leave Sunderland,' Darren says. 'Reidy just called me in one day and told me that he had accepted a bid from Wimbledon and that he wanted me to go and speak to them. I had no intention of speaking to them. I was a northerner and I didn't want to go and live in London. I talked to my agent about it and he encouraged me to speak to them as well.

'I saw Reidy again and I told him that I really didn't want to leave. He then told me he wasn't going to play me. I told him that I would play in the reserves. He told me he wouldn't play me in the reserves. I lost my rag. I started calling him a few words that weren't nice. But I was angry and it had all come from out of the blue. Bearing in mind what I had seen happen with Michael Bridges and Allan Johnston at Sunderland [Bridges and Johnston were transfer-listed by Peter Reid on the same day in the summer of 1999 during protracted contract talks. Despite both players being integral parts of the record-breaking 105-point season, neither of them played for Sunderland again], which was not nice to see, I knew that I couldn't do that. I knew that I would end up blowing my top. He remained adamant. There was no first-team football, no reserve-team football, and he wouldn't give me a reason. What could I do? I was stuck. I needed to play football.'

By now an England Under-21 international, Holloway signed for Wimbledon for £1.2 million. His target was to return to the Premier League as soon as possible.

'Wimbledon had just been relegated from the Premier League, but they still had some really good players, like John Hartson, Jason Euell and Damien Francis. I spoke to Terry Burton, who was the manager at the time, and I got shown around by the chief executive. I remember that we drove past a David Lloyd club and there was a non-league stadium nearby and he told me that they were going to buy that and turn all this grass into a training pitch. They looked like they were going to pump some money into it, so I thought that they must have strong ambitions to get back into the Premier League and I signed for them.

'We finished eighth but we were good enough to get into the play-offs,' Darren recalls. 'Then, the following season, the alarm bells started ringing. All the big earners were on the move, all the talk of the stadium went up in the air, Terry Burton lost his job and the club went into administration. Then Pete Winkelman came along and we ended up moving to Milton Keynes. Obviously, he had his own ambitions for the club and it has turned out well for him, but I remember we played Rotherham United on a Tuesday night at Selhurst Park and there were about 600 people there. The fans boycotted the match over the forthcoming move to Milton Keynes, which was understandable as it was about 50 miles up the road from where they were. I didn't want to go to Milton Keynes. We even played in the national hockey stadium there for a while. I was living in Surrey and it took me three hours to get to a game on one occasion due to a traffic jam on the M25 and I missed the kick-off. I got a knee injury towards the end of my contract there and I decided I just wanted to leave and come back up north.

'What curtailed my career towards the end were too many knee injuries. I have had five operations on my right knee and four on my left knee. Once you get the first one and then you go in again for another one you know that everything is not going to be hunky dory. So it was something of a downward slope for me.

'I went to Bradford City and played for Colin Todd. Then Darlington came in for me. They were in League Three at the time and I didn't want to drop down there, but I liked David Hodgson as a bloke and it was close to home. I thought we could get promoted. Alun Armstrong was there and he was our top scorer, but we under-achieved, the manager got the sack, Dave Penney came in and he squeezed me out. I went to Stockport, but they couldn't afford me. So I then went to Bury and I played centre-half in this practice game and as I passed the ball to the player alongside me, I shouted "time" and he just booted the ball out of play! He said to me, "That's not my game, just get it up field!" That sickened me. I thought, "I can't be chasing around trying to get a contract to play alongside people like that." It finished me as a professional. I fell out of love with it. I came home and I didn't do anything for about a year.

'It was Ian Bogie, at Gateshead, who eventually pestered me into training with them. I enjoyed it up there and so I signed for them. They got promoted into the National League. But we trained on 3G and my knees didn't like it and they started to give me grief again. So I left. I knew I couldn't play football regularly for them.

'Mick Tait wanted to sign me for Blyth Spartans, but I still didn't feel right. In the end I had an operation and it turned out to be a lot worse than the surgeon originally thought it was. That was a kick in the teeth for me because I thought I could get fixed. I still like to join in, but I shouldn't do it, really. I miss playing football badly, but coaching is probably the next best thing.'

And it is at Blyth Spartans, one of the most famous non-league clubs in the country after their glorious run to the fifth round of the FA Cup in 1978, that Holloway is now experiencing his first taste of coaching in senior football.

'I never saw myself coming out of football,' Darren says. 'I was always a good communicator on the pitch and so I thought that the coaching side was something that I needed to do. I did the FA Level 2 coaching course and the UEFA B Licence. Once I had that it meant I could coach in the academies, so I spoke to Kevin Ball and he put a word in with Ged McNamee at Sunderland. But I heard nothing. I just got a letter in the post saying there were no vacancies. That left a really sour taste in my mouth. My photograph is still up in the academy there so I had hoped for something better than that. I spent a year with the Under-11s at Hartlepool and then progressed to the Under-13s, and then I went to Middlesbrough to work for their academy. I enjoyed my time in the academies, but I had to knock it on the head when I got my job at Blyth.

'Initially, I wasn't going to do it,' Darren explains. 'Alun Armstrong was working at the Middlesbrough academy at the same time as me and we knew each other from our time together at Darlington anyway. He collared me in the car park one day and offered me the job as his assistant at Blyth. I went up to watch them and I thought it was a really good set-up. It was also like a breath of fresh air for me: playing competitive matches rather than working in development. I got a buzz for it. Don't get me wrong, academy work is great, but it doesn't give you the nitty-gritty of football that we all love so much.

'We got promoted from the Northern Premier League into the National League North last season, which was great for us,' Darren adds. 'This season is a big challenge at a higher level. We are ambitious people and our hope is that maybe we can do so well that someone spots us or perhaps an investor comes along who wants to pump millions of pounds into it and we can kick on.'

Back in 1978, only a fallen corner flag and subsequent last-minute equaliser at Wrexham prevented Blyth from sensationally reaching the FA Cup quarter-finals. Roker Park was lined up to host a last-eight encounter against Arsenal had they got through the fifth-round replay. Sadly Blyth lost 2-1 in front of 42,167 fans at St James' Park.

But that amazing cup run – which featured Sunderland's 1973 FA Cup hero Ron Guthrie at left-back – created a legacy that means that whenever the club comes anywhere close to achieving success again it generates national interest. As happened three years ago, when BBC One showed live coverage of the club's FA Cup second-round win at Hartlepool United.

'We have had a bit of the spotlight recently with the team doing so well in the FA Cup and the cameras coming along,' Darren says. 'We want to do well in the league and become established at this level, but we would obviously love a good cup run to generate some money as well. We want to win every game. Also, if we are selfish, it would put us out there and who knows what could happen?'

It is sometimes said that football is cyclical. Well, Blyth began their most famous FA Cup run back in the summer of 1977 and, in early October, they played at Crook Town just five days after Holloway was born. It is nothing more than a coincidence, of course, but it is a nice line to conclude the interview.

'The Blyth fans still talk about those glory days,' Darren says. 'They would like to have those days back again. But we have to put things in perspective: we play in a league with teams that are full-time and who are paying good money for players.

'For me, football will always be defined by money. The Premier League will probably be defined by the best budgets again this season. I don't think we will see what happened with Leicester City happening again in my lifetime. If you show me the five biggest budgets in our league, I will probably pick you the five best teams in the league. It is that simple. We have just got to find our feet and compete. But, you never know . . .'

3

For too many years left-back has been a problem position at Sunderland.

It wasn't when **Martin Scott** was there.

He was honest, fearless and direct as a player – just as he is in this chapter, looking back on a career which included being forced out of Bristol City and arriving at a Sunderland Football Club in complete disarray.

Revival began with Reid, the history books tell us, but Scott suggests player power might have started the upturn even before the inspirational manager arrived to put an end to the depressing Mick Buxton era.

Scott's eventful Sunderland stay took in unlikely promotion and agonising relegation; play-off heartbreak and a record-breaking points' total; as well as the switch from Roker Park to the Stadium of Light before injuries curtailed his career with his peak years potentially still ahead.

MARTIN SCOTT

MEETS GRAEME ANDERSON

On any given Sunday, Martin Scott prepares coaching lessons for talented young kids who hope to be among the next generation of pro footballers in the north-east.

On any given weekday, he's on the training pitch with elite prospects trying to do what his Improtech Soccer Football Academy subtly says on the label: Improve Technique.

Almost two decades since he reluctantly hung up his boots, amid feelings of anguish, depression and no small amount of anger, Scott looks lean and sharp enough to still be playing – the 48-year-old's hair remains trademark jet black, though friends and former teammates tease him.

'It's not dyed,' he says, with a Sphinx-like smile.

Out in training, the UEFA Pro Licence holder coaches and coaxes the best out of kids at Kepier Academy, Hartlepool Martyrs, Sunderland College and South Shields FC Football Academy. But whatever centre he's at the message is always the same: you need tenacity, every bit as much as you need talent.

In that regard, although coaching may be business for him, it's also personal.

That's because Scott's playing career – from Rotherham United to Bristol City and Sunderland; from the Fourth Division to the Premier League – had more than its fair share of triumph over adversity, and the need to be mentally strong is something he constantly drives home to his young charges:

'I ask them, "Do you want to be a footballer or do you NEED to be a footballer?"' he says, as we chat in a featureless office in Sunderland College's smart new £1 million sports centre. 'That's because unless you have that desperate desire and drive, you're not going to make it.'

Scott needed to be a footballer from as early as he can remember and by the time he arrived at Roker Park in January 1994, having just turned 26, he had overcome more adversity than most.

Always pictured with a ball growing up in Sheffield, always out watching games with dad Fred, he was football-obsessed, but his first barrier was not his hunger for the game, but his height.

'I was the smallest right through the grass roots teams,' he says. 'I didn't grow until later. I was 5 foot 2 inches, 5 foot 3 inches at 15 – really small. So I had all the "not big enough" stuff thrown at me, as kids still do today. But that summer, right after leaving school, I grew: it was like putting a pair of trousers on and growing two inches, it was that quick.'

That growth spurt, coupled with a natural athleticism and a genuine talent, saw him break into Rotherham United's first team at just 17. He was handed his debut by George Kerr, brother of FA Cup-winning Sunderland captain Bobby. But with only a few games under his belt, he suddenly faced a rare and career-threatening medical condition.

'I was getting really bad pains in my legs and the doctors discovered my pelvis was still moving inside my body at an age when it shouldn't have been,' he reveals. 'I faced a big decision: total rest for 12 months and no guarantees, or an operation where they took a piece of bone from your hip and pinned it to your pelvis with two big screws. It was a massive, massive operation but it could get you back sooner and I opted to go for that.

'It was a nightmare time and I was out for eight months. I felt my career was on the rocks before it had even started. But I gave everything to rehabilitation, and times like that – giving everything morning to night – helped make me the person I am.'

When he returned to training again, more determined than ever, Scott found not just form and fitness but the position on the pitch that was to bring the best out of him. Regular left-back Phil Crosby suffered an injury and the youngster was asked to stand in at full-back.

'I was a central midfielder up to that point,' Scott recalls. 'But I was the only left-footed option at the club at the time. So I moved to left-back and I immediately found it really suited me, so much so that I held my place for the rest of my time at Rotherham, eventually playing more than 100 odd games at left-back.

'I realised pretty quickly that I wasn't a midfielder – only my energy was getting me by in midfield – and once I started to play at left-back, where everything was in front of me rather than receiving it with your back to goal a lot of the time, I knew I was going to flourish. My energy driving forward, my left foot, my passing – I loved it.'

This was when Scott's career finally began a smooth upward trajectory. Scoring a memorable free-kick against an Everton side in the 1987 League Cup – the shot from 25 yards beating Neville Southall as Peter Reid looked on – helped raise the profile of the young prospect. He was linked with Glasgow Rangers and Everton and went on loan to Brian Clough's Nottingham Forest. At one point, certain that he was going to be offered a move to the City Ground, he was recalled by the struggling Millers. Out of contract at one stage at Millmoor, he turned down a move to a Neil Warnock-led Notts County side which were bound for the top flight.

'I just thought after Rotherham had stood by me over the surgery and everything else. They deserved a bit of loyalty,' Scott explains.

Eventually Rotherham cashed in on that loyalty, selling the defender to Bristol City for £200,000 – a move which was fine by the player himself.

'I made the club money and I was happy about that, but I was ready to move on and Bristol City were a much bigger club – bigger tradition, bigger fan base – and I loved it there,' said Scott. 'My first game we played against Sheffield Wednesday and Trevor Francis was the right-winger under Ron Atkinson. All the talk was about this ex-England international but I won man of the match that day against him. I hit the ground running at City. It was a good club and things went really smoothly for me the four years I was there, forming a good partnership with ex-Newcastle United winger Brian Tinnion down the left.

'I had four managers in four years at Bristol, including ex-Sunderland boss Denis Smith, but when Joe Jordan arrived as boss, I knew I was on my way,' he says. 'His back was against the wall, he needed money and I was his biggest asset, but I felt he could have done it differently – he made my life difficult because he wanted me to go. I've met him many times since and he explained why he did it – he was going to get £450,000 from Sunderland and Gary Owers, who was a decent player, in exchange for me. He could utilise that money and potentially keep Bristol City in the league because, like Sunderland, we were both struggling at the wrong end of the Championship – but for me, Joe might have done it differently.'

Unhappy with Jordan, Scott headed to the opposite end of the country in December 1994, ready to leave Ashton Gate if Sunderland struck him as the right move. But talks did not go smoothly and Scott reveals for the first time how he was virtually strong-armed into the deal.

'I met Sunderland manager Mick Buxton in Doncaster for a quick hour before going up to Sunderland the next day for negotiations,' he says. 'I knew nothing about Sunderland, not even that it was by the sea, or that at that time of year it could be so cold! I had negotiations, they didn't go well. I turned it down and went back to the hotel at Seaburn, the Marriott.

'Then the phone rang in my room. Joe Jordan. "How's negotiations going?" "Not well, I'm travelling back tomorrow. I'm not going to sign."

"You f***ing well are," says Joe.

"No I'm not."

"Yes you are," says Joe. "I've done an article in the local paper – it's headlines tonight – you've asked to leave, the fans won't accept you any more."

'And that was that,' shrugs Scott. 'That's how football can be – dog-eat-dog.

'So Mick Buxton came back around. We were £10,000 apart and eventually we met in the middle and it became £5,000 and I signed the contract.

'Once I'd signed, I was never going to sulk. I was always going to give 100 per cent to Sunderland, that's in my nature.

'But mentally it was a tough period because of how the transfer had gone about and because of how my confidence had been affected at Bristol.

'It's funny how things work. Now, I absolutely love Sunderland and it turned out to be a wonderful move for me and my family, but I would not have joined if I'd been allowed to have my own way after those talks.'

It was time for Scott to adjust to his changed circumstances and win over fans at his new club – a club which had lost its way and was being haunted by the prospect of dropping into the old Third Division for only the second time in its history. It did not start well.

Scott's debut in a forgettable Boxing Day game against Bolton Wanderers saw the defender struggling to hit the ground running, as he had done at Ashton Gate.

'I was thrown in at the deep end and in my first game I was absolutely woeful,' he says with a shake of the head. 'It was a real tough game for me and I was lacking confidence and belief. My dad's honest, and when I went into the players' lounge afterwards he wouldn't talk to me – just literally refused to talk. My mam was lost for words too. So how bad must I have been?'

It wasn't just Scott's lack of confidence, though: Sunderland were struggling terribly with morale rock-bottom across the board. It felt like there was a sickness in the club. The left-back had been parachuted into a mess not of his own making with the Black Cats' management deeply unpopular with both players and fans and clueless as to how to stop the slide. There was another awkwardly timed aspect to Scott's arrival too.

'They were in a really tough position, sliding down the table, when I arrived and they had also just sold their star striker Don Goodman,' says Scott. 'All the speculation was about who would replace him and score the goals to get them out of relegation trouble. Then, against that background, Mick Buxton signs a left-back! "Left-back? LEFT-BACK? We've sold our star striker to Wolves for £1 million and signed a *left-back?!* So I had all this going on in my head and the atmosphere in the dressing room wasn't good either. Kevin Ball came up to me at the Charlie Hurley Centre in the first few days, pointed at me and said, "First impressions?"

'And I said, "Relegation. No standards, unprofessional and too many players hate the manager."

'And he looked at me and said, "Spot on, mate. Absolutely spot on."

'Bally and me are firm friends to this day, and that was the start of it. We've always been honest with each other and after that first conversation we started to grow close and talk and things started to improve. The Richard Ords, the Andy Melvilles, Mickey Grays, Martin Smiths – good, talented players but so disillusioned – started to think again. Steve Agnew was brought in and we shared the same hotel together, started to get to know each other and we started to get a good mindset.

'The slump proved hard to stop though – within a few games of my arrival Sunderland were in the relegation zone and Bristol City had leapfrogged us: how do you think that made me feel at the time?' says Scott.

Buxton left and Peter Reid, who arrived soon afterwards, was credited with the miracle of turning the club around in their last seven games and saving them from the drop.

But for Scott, the team-spirit which was to serve the team so well the following season, pre-dated the Liverpudlian's arrival.

He said, 'Reidy really galvanised us but to me the key was a team meeting we held in the dressing room shortly before his arrival. Me and Bally organised it and Bally led it with everyone voicing their own concerns and opinions, and it helped us, it really did. We started to understand each other and then Peter Reid got the job, added to what we spoke about, brought Sacko in, and the manager just started to treat people right, get them on board.'

Reid's first game in charge, against Sheffield United, required a breathless, last-minute goal from Craig Russell in front of the Fulwell End to get the new manager off to a winning start. But momentum and belief grew rapidly and safety was sealed in the penultimate game of the season, at Turf Moor.

'The Burnley game was massive – a massive away following, massive game – we got the point we needed and Reidy played a big part in that,' said Scott. 'We were just walking out of the dressing room, all het up, and Reidy said, "Right, lads, I'm going to tell you a joke." And he started telling this joke about a snail – I think it was a snail knocking on a door; and I'd heard it before – but it was a long drawn-out joke with a real good ending. And we were all wetting ourselves laughing two minutes before kick-off. We were crying with laughing and it took all the pressure off us – it was a great bit of management.'

Survival ensured that the decision for a proposed new super stadium at Wearmouth would remain on the table, and Reid set about trying to construct a team worthy of it. The fans who had followed in such numbers at Roker were revived.

'A lot of changes happened,' nods Scott. 'Reidy wasn't daft and he knew there had to be changes. He brought in Paul Bracewell, who was a key signing, got rid of players too, and suddenly the back four became established: me, Ordy, Melville, Dariusz.'

That defensive platform – right-back Dariusz Kubicki, centre-halves Andy Melville and Richard Ord (with Kevin Ball occasionally filling in), and left-back Martin Scott were to be the rearguard on which promotion was built in the 1995-96 season, with Alec Chamberlain and Shay Given behind them in goal over the course of the campaign. Considering what had gone before, it was one of the most unlikely, and one of the most inspiring of Sunderland's promotions. And it was to be based on a team that kept consistently picking up points thanks to that miserly defence. By the season's end, more than a dozen clubs in the league would score more goals than Sunderland that year – even relegated Watford scored more! – but the side with the second best defensive record to Sunderland that season had conceded a whopping dozen more goals. In all, Sunderland were to pick the ball out of the back of the net just 33 times in 46 games – a figure that included a club-record 26 clean sheets.

'We weren't the best ability-wise in the division but we would run through a brick wall for each other,' points out Scott. 'We were well-drilled – 4-4-2; didn't do anything else – and we knew how to play against other formations. It was real basic stuff and built on a massive respect among the back four. The clean sheets were incredible because they gave us confidence and they gave us pride – some teams revel in how many goals they score, we took pride in how many we stopped. We had been a bit of a soft touch previously, but no more, and we evolved into a defensive unit that would do anything for each other. We were never prolific but as a team we just ground out results week after week.

'Pre-season had been fantastic: Reidy brought some new ideas in, he loved his weekends away with the lads, and he treated us like adults.'

The initial signs were not great, however. Sunderland were in the bottom half of the table after the first four games but gradually that mean defence provided the platform for points to be accumulated on a regular basis. And as the shadows lengthened towards the end of the year, Sunderland inched their way just as gradually up the table.

In a long and demanding season, two games stand out for Scott – the 6-0 victory over Millwall in December, where he scored the opening goal, and the 4-0 win over Grimsby Town in March – each game for very different reasons.

'We were picking up results but we knew we weren't the most skilful side in the division and we weren't a side to score stacks of goals,' said Scott. 'But I think the Millwall game was the one which really gave us belief we could go up. Millwall looked good for promotion when they came to Roker Park but we hammered them and they went into such a fall afterwards that they ended up being relegated.'

Scott settled his side, putting them ahead from the penalty spot, though this was far from his most assured moment.

'I liked taking penalties, I always felt confident on them,' he recalls. 'My family would make good money on me over the course of the season betting for me to be on the scoresheet. The bookies never seemed to take into account that I took penalties – only that I was a defender – and I would regularly be 25-1 or more to score, which meant quite a few paydays!'

Scott scored six goals that season, four of them from the penalty spot, the left-back finishing as his side's third top goalscorer.

But the Millwall penalty was possibly the most contentious and crucial of his goals – just as important in its own way as his match-winners against Crystal Palace and Oldham Athletic that season. Scott's opening goal against the Lions ignited the 6-0 goal fest in which Craig Russell notched four, but it was words of wisdom from assistant manager Bobby Saxton which set Sunderland on their way.

'We loved Sacko,' grins Scot. 'He was a real character, old school, and I still see him now – real, honest professional who really knew his stuff. Before the Millwall game he shouted over to me to put the ball in the opposite corner to what I'd normally do if we got a penalty. I was completely confused, but he explained that he'd heard Millwall keeper Kasey Keller always watched videos of where his opponent's penalty-takers normally put their shots before a game so he knew which way to dive.

'It annoyed me at the time because I felt he'd put a doubt in my mind. I always went to the keeper's left but now I wasn't so sure.

'Sure enough, we got a penalty against Millwall early on and I changed it – that was the only time I changed it in my career – I listened to Sacko in my mind and went right instead of left.

'And I'm glad I did because Kasey Keller went the other way and I played it across him. I turned around to celebrate and all I could see was Sacko jumping around and laughing on the bench because he'd been right, his homework had paid off! We went on to absolutely hammer Millwall that game and that took our confidence to a whole new level.

'The Grimsby game a few months later sticks out in my mind for completely different reasons.

'We were terrible that day and we got a tongue-lashing at half-time but we went on to win the game 4-0.

'We were actually going to Mottram Hall for three or four days afterwards and were really looking forward to it, but Reidy and Sacko were fuming after the game. Reidy ripped into Bally and it kicked off again that night at Mottram Hall, Sacko having a go at Bally because Bally was suggesting that, even though we'd played rubbish, at least we'd won.

'But that's how they were as a management team. They were winners and they were unhappy that even though we'd won the game, we hadn't done it right.

'We were to realise later that Reidy and Sacko knew that if they had a go at the main men, we'd take it the right way and be positive and that would encourage the younger and more vulnerable players without hitting their confidence.

'The point was that it was March and we were on course for promotion, but maybe we'd got complacent and were believing our own publicity, letting our standards drop. Winning at Grimsby might have disguised that but the management feared it and were utterly determined to guard against it.'

Despite the occasional verbal battering, this was far and away Scott's favourite season as a player.

'We were just such a team, in every sense of the word,' he said. 'We all had our places and would do anything to help each other. Usually that meant Ordy and Melville battering Darius throughout a game and me acting as a peacekeeper!

'But in front of us we had Bally and Bracewell in midfield offering protection to our defence and Mickey Gray ahead of me on the left-flank covered so much ground he made my life a lot easier. On top of that you had people like Steve Agnew, playing out of position on the right wing for the sake of the team but still contributing.

'Everything about that team was about us being a team – it couldn't have been a bigger contrast to how it was when I was first signed.'

By the turn of the year Sunderland were gaining ground in the promotion chase and, with a sense of renewal and positivity in the air, they faced Manchester United in January in an FA Cup game they almost certainly would have won had keeper Alec Chamberlain not dropped a cross right in front of, of all people, Eric Cantona. Though Alec Chamberlain's goal concession average wasn't too bad that season, the shocker against Man United saw him dropped, and that gave a platform for unknown teenager Shay Given, Blackburn Rovers' on-loan reserve team keeper.

We all know now, of course, that Given was a star in the making. But, at the time, his astonishing form boosted both the players and, just as importantly, helped propel Sunderland into the promotion places as that mean defence got even meaner.

'Shay was great,' says Scott. 'He was this unknown kid but he played with so much freedom and belief. We had a fantastic back four but he brought something different to us.

'It was just a great time to be involved in every way because you could see this great club coming more and more back to life. Michael Bridges was a phenomenon when he came on the scene, a supersub coming on, scoring goals; Mickey Gray, Martin Smith, Craig Russell, all these young players suddenly came to the party. Reidy had said everybody's slate was clean, and they took advantage of it in a big way and it took us to a different level. I was really pleased about that because previously I'd honestly wondered what would happen to all these young lads. As it was, they just grew in confidence.

'Reidy deserves credit for keeping us up and getting us up but I do think that the group chat we had, the togetherness we created that day the previous season was so important in terms of the bonds the honesty created.

'Reidy undoubtedly galvanised us though, and to go from just missing out on relegation to the third tier, to being a Premier League team a year later, was incredible.

'The feel-good factor just increased, as did our confidence, and we rose up the league month by month until in the end we won it quite comfortably.

'It was the season of "Cheer Up, Peter Reid", and the whole thing just put the smiles back on the faces of Sunderland fans.'

As a journalist covering the club closely for the *Sunderland Echo*, I can remember the wave of positivity which gradually built over the course of the campaign. Peter Reid ran an open training ground with reporters allowed – in fact, encouraged – to develop good relationships with the players. And the group of press, waiting for interviews at the Charlie Hurley Centre in Whitburn come rain or shine could vouch for the sense of fun around the place. You could often hear peals of laughter ringing around the portable cabins before you even saw a member of the playing staff. And Scott, always the joker, was regularly at the heart of the banter and the mickey-taking. He was a natural live-wire character and while he took his football deadly seriously, he threw himself with equal commitment into the social side of the job, where skipper Kevin Ball was forever trying to keep a dressing room full of strong characters and differing senses of humour under control.

Having started his Sunderland career with a shaky debut, Scot's dependability and enterprise had by now made him a crowd favourite.

'I quickly recognised what Sunderland fans liked in a player and I was lucky – the qualities they liked in a player was me, through and through,' he says. 'I love football: I love watching it, I love playing it, I love reading about it . . . and Sunderland fans are the same. I think that's why I was well liked – maybe also because I loved to get stuck in!

'But I'm always made welcome now when I go back and I love going back.'

The following season, 1996-97, Roker Park's first and only season in the Premier League, was to stand in contrast to what had gone before: a top-flight season with some special highlights – wins over Everton, Chelsea, Arsenal and Manchester United – but one which was to end in personal disappointment for Scott and collective heartbreak for Sunderland fans.

'We moved forward: exciting times behind the scenes, we knew what was happening with the club, Roker Park, changing grounds,' says Scott. 'To get promoted the year before we moved to the Stadium of Light and to have a full season at Roker Park was great. The TV cameras were following us around for the series *Premier Passions* and we really felt up for it.'

Sunderland had strengthened with the signings of Niall Quinn and Tony Coton and, to Scott, the familiar face of former opponent Alex Rae.

'The season I left Bristol, Alex had tried to headbutt me at Ashton Gate and got sent off,' smiles Scott. 'He's the sort of player I played against numerous times and we hated each other. We were constantly having a go at each other, mouthing off, but he was one of those players you would love playing on your side. And when he eventually signed for Sunderland, I had a little chuckle to myself. Alex was a good lad, great character, and I never fell out with him once. I think the world of him. He's had his issues along the way, but what a fantastic player – and the players Reidy signed that summer all looked as though they would make us stronger and able to compete.'

That certainly looked to be the case as the season got off to a solid start, but soon Coton, Scott and Quinn were sidelined by serious injuries, and the promising opening proved increasingly difficult to sustain. Along the way, Scott scored Sunderland's first ever Premier League derby goal against Newcastle United, but while fellow Sunderland full-back Patrice Carteron's goal against the Magpies a few years later is still celebrated, Scott's seems almost forgotten. When Sunderland fans approach him these days they'll congratulate him for his ability and his style of play, they usually mention that first promotion season, but the derby goal rarely merits a mention.

'I understand why,' says Scott. 'It was a wonderful moment at the time to see the ball hit the back of the net – an evening kick-off at Roker Park and an early first-half penalty which I put past Pavel Srníček, the home crowd going wild. But we conceded two goals in the second half, and there was a horrible atmosphere because it was also that season when away fans were banned from the derby games, and it really made for a mean mood in the ground. I think that's a derby fans have pretty much wiped from their memory.'

The derby defeat at Roker Park was to be one of the disappointments in what would prove to be a relegation season, albeit an agonisingly close demotion, the Black Cats dropping through the trapdoor on the very last day of the campaign; the first team to be relegated after reaching the 40-point milestone.

'People forget we were mid-table in January,' says Scott. 'We were so unlucky in so many ways but particularly with key injuries.'

Scott was one of those.

The defender, voted Player of the Month by *Sunderland Echo* readers in September, injured himself in November leaping for a ball against Leeds United, suffering an ankle injury which meant he barely played again for the remainder of the campaign.

'I played only about 15 league games that season and was always struggling to get back and Dariusz and Gareth Hall had to be our full-backs for most of the season, which wasn't ideal. It was a frustrating time because I was a Premier League player injured when the club was fighting for its life.'

A personal heartache for Scott though was the realisation that an injury-free season could have led to an England call-up.

He recalls, 'I'd had such a good season in the promotion campaign and I started well in the Premier League and I heard rumours that England were looking at me. It was an interesting time to be a left-back because Stuart Pearce was 34 going on 35 and they were looking around for contenders. I had a long talk, when I was on crutches at Roker Park, with someone who pretty much confirmed I was in the reckoning for a call-up – the conversation was all about how serious the injury was and how long it would be before I got back.

'Several years later, Mickey Gray got call-ups as England continued to look at that left-back position, and while I was glad for him I'll always wonder if in different circumstances it might have been me a season or two earlier.'

Relegation came against Wimbledon when the disinterested Dons reluctantly scuffed their way to a 1-0 win over a Sunderland side utterly shot of confidence.

'The trip to Wimbledon, last game of the season, was horrible because we were crying out for a goal but couldn't get one for love nor money,' Scott remembers. 'You could sense that Wimbledon weren't really bothered. But we just froze on the day and they scrambled a goal home almost apologetically. It was a horrible atmosphere and it was all the worse because we had started the season well and were holding our own. Defensively we were strong, though we were never prolific, and it didn't look too bad until mid-February.'

The injury to Scott continued to prove troublesome, failing to completely clear up over the close season and, with injuries starting to mount up, he rarely got a run in the side in his last two seasons.

Other senior players who had previously gained promotion were also struggling and Reid rang the changes within months of the start of the 1997-98 season, preferring youthful players, who helped galvanise performances again.

That left Scott time to rest and recuperate, but also saw Mickey Gray begin to establish himself at left-back as the Yorkshireman stopped being first-choice for the first time since his arrival.

'It was tough,' says Scott. 'I started the season with niggling injuries and a 4-0 defeat to Reading in October saw the manager have a right go at us as a back four. We were all carrying knocks or out of form. I got injured against Reading and Mickey Gray, realistically, took my place, and full credit to the younger players who came in, they took it on. They were naïve in certain areas but they had bags of energy and started to play some really good football.'

By this stage, of course, Sunderland were playing in a wonderful new arena and Scotty loved it, though he would have preferred more game time.

'It was the first season at the Stadium of Light and I was a spectator for much of it but we were all amazed by how great a stadium it was. Eventually we got to the play-offs having played some absolutely amazing football, and then the play-off final was such a roller coaster of a day, which ended in that crushing disappointment.

'I was really frustrated at the time: I was still injured, I'd played games that year I probably shouldn't have done, but I was so desperate to get back. The play-off defeat was crushing but, like the rest of the squad, I was determined to come back stronger than ever the following season. The problem was that by this time I was fighting injuries constantly. I was struggling big-style. I'd had two major operations on my ankle and I never recovered from that.'

Scott still managed to play the opening game of the 1998-99 season, a 1-0 victory over QPR, and would play 22 more times before the end of the year, when injury once again forced him out.

'The 105-pointers,' says Scott, noting the record points total at the time of any side in English football that Sunderland achieved that season. 'The great thing was that we had two good players for every position, and I think that can't be overlooked,' he points out. 'People remember Mickey and Allan Johnston down the left that season, and rightly so, they were amazing, but I played most of the first half of the season and it was the same all the way through the side where the manager had options to call on. Niall Quinn and Kevin Phillips were fantastic up front, for example, but Mickey Bridges and Danny Dichio also made vital contributions. It was a great team effort from a proper squad when we were winning all those games, so as well as the obvious first-teamers, there were plenty of contributions from many others who came in and played games.'

Alas, Scott's Sunderland contribution was almost over.

He suffered an innocuous but devastating injury against Lincoln in January 1999 in one of the most forgettable FA Cup games of all time. I was there in the press box as one of the worst games of football I've ever reported on was distinguished by a scuffed Gavin McCann winner, typical of the scrappy nature of the game, and an injury to Scott – one which, though seemingly occurring out of nothing, you sensed was a bad one.

'I'd struggled with the Leeds injury but the Lincoln game – which injured the other ankle – was the final straw,' he accepts.

Like many a footballer recalling a fateful day, Scott wonders if it might all have turned out differently.

'The Lincoln game . . . we got to the ground and the pitch was woeful,' he remembers. 'For some reason we got there late, got back to the dressing room late, and I'd been having a bit of niggle in my ankle and I'd had every intention putting a stirrup strapping on it to give me some reassurance. But because we were late, Reidy was talking, I just thought I wouldn't bother, so bang, just put the sock straight back on again.

'And the injury happened in such a trivial incident – a throw-in down the line. I jumped and as I came down I caught the lad's foot, so I landed awkwardly with my full weight on my ankle. I was taken to hospital by ambulance and was told there's no break, but I knew there was: my ankle was enormous. "No," they were insistent, so I came back to the ground on crutches for the last 10 minutes. When I got back home I was rushed into Washington Hospital where they X-rayed it the next day, put cameras and stuff in there and confirmed I'd broken the lower part of the leg and totally ruptured my ankle ligaments. It was a bad one, a complicated one.'

Faced with another challenge, Scott threw himself, in typical style, into his rehab, displaying the determination which had carried him so far in his career.

'Bally used to say I took rehab to another level, but I was determined to fight all the way,' said Scott. 'I went to rehab in Lilleshall for 13 weeks. Normally you only go for one or two, but I lived away from my family for 13 weeks, I was so focused. I was the fittest I had ever been and I knew I had to be because my contract was up at the end of that season.

'Would I have got into the first team the way Sunderland were playing towards the end of that promotion season? Probably not. But I was working towards the next season and I'd heard word the club wanted me to battle it out with Mickey for the left-back position over the next couple of seasons.' Disappointment came out of the blue for Scott, when the manager called him into his office and told him he had decided to go for youth and that Scott's contract would not be renewed.

'It was such a shock, just before the 1998-99 season finished, and I went, "Oh My God!" It hit me like a ton of bricks because I just could not see me playing for another club. I'd had four seasons there and I loved the club. It hit me hard and, for that reason, I didn't really feel part of the end-of-season celebrations when promotion back to the Premier League was confirmed.'

Plenty of clubs came calling for Scott, more than a dozen, despite his injury problems. The club which led the chase was Ipswich Town, then managed by former Sunderland right-back George Burley, but it was newly promoted Bradford City who won Scott's signature.

'Manager Paul Jewell was gearing up for the Premier League and he wanted me. He told me he'd bid £1 million for me in [the previous] January and he was delighted now to get me for nothing,' the left-back recounts. 'They offered me a three-year contract – I was still only 30, remember – and I was looking forward to playing with Benito Carbone and co.

'But there were problems with my medical. Jewell called me in and said scans had revealed I had nothing holding my ankle together – the doctors were amazed I was running.

'I fought my corner and said, "Let's see how it goes preseason, and if it breaks down, I will walk away."

'But when we stepped up the work level I collapsed in training, they operated, put cameras in and the next morning advised me to retire. You know what I'm like: I wouldn't give up and I knew there was a £25,000 operation – a reconstruction and a rebuild – that might give me a chance. I rang Sunderland up, hoping they would help – after all, I'd damaged it playing for them – but they wouldn't, and that was when me and Reidy fell out because he refused to help because I had signed for Bradford. Nothing materialised from Sunderland so I rang up the PFA and the surgeon I'd heard about and eventually paid for it myself. I got half of it back from the PFA – though I didn't know that would happen at the time – and was left wondering, "Now what?"'

Non-league Doncaster Rovers offered him a pay-as-you-play deal and Scott went to Hartlepool to train under Chris Turner to get fit, but opportunity knocked when a vacancy came up for a youth-team coach at Victoria Park and he took it.

'I had to make a decision and I knew the ankle wasn't right, so I took the job and retired as a pro footballer.'

Scars, of course, can be mental as well as physical, and the consequences of those injuries affected him on many levels.

'It's a lonely time, when you're injured, and I had so much of that at the end of my career,' he says. 'Every time I got injured I went into total overdrive rehab. I was a fitness fanatic and I was horrible to live with. If I'm honest, that time has affected me long-term and I still struggle with it now. I look back on my career, and every single season I had to fight for it.

'And that is what has made me so determined to go into my coaching the way I do and look to prepare and support and get the best out of every player.' Scott tried his hand at just about every coaching and managerial position there was after retiring but found that his calling lay in coaching and developing elite young players capable of making it into the professional ranks with the right sort of guidance.

'When I look back on my career, despite all the good times, the championship medals and the knowledge that with the pelvic injury it could have been all over before it began, I still feel a little robbed,' he says. 'As a young player I'd always wanted to play at the top level, and I got chances to do that at Sunderland and at the Stadium of Light. My dreams were all starting to come true but then to lose that, to have it taken away from you, it hits you harder. I had a fantastic time at every club I was at, but I feel like injuries cost me so many games and so many good times. I think I could have carried on until I was 36, 37, 38, because I was a fit, fit lad, but I retired at 30 and I think I could have reached a higher level too. It's probably the typical footballer's regret: always what might have beens, rather than what was.

'All my experiences, though, have made me better as a coach and as a manager. I have so much experience to pass on to young lads, especially when they are injured or improving and getting to a higher level. I channel a lot of my energies into the kids and I love to see them progress. I'm passionate about that and that's the way I am – I was the same as a player.'

And with that, Scott is out of the cramped office at Sunderland College and off to check on the young hopefuls on the training pitch. I can't help but feel that his current vocation is the one which suits him best – teaching and supporting and instilling the burning desire which carried him so far for so long in his own career. As he bounds out of the office he looks happy, a lot younger than his 48 years, and I tell him so.

'Thanks,' he says, grinning. 'It's not dyed, by the way.'

4

Stan Anderson saw a lot in his 14 years at Sunderland.

He played under Bill Murray and Alan Brown, and played alongside Len Shackleton and Brian Clough.

He was part of the first Sunderland side ever to be relegated, and then captained the club to the FA Cup quarter-finals just a few years later.

He was present at the time when Sunderland were known as the 'Bank of England club' and then watched helplessly as it collapsed around him. He won England caps and went to the 1962 World Cup in Chile.

His story is a fascinating tale of experiencing success, heartache and genius.

STAN ANDERSON

MEETS LANCE HARDY

Former Sunderland captain Stan Anderson is now aged 83; the fact that he looks much younger could be explained by the fact that he just finished the first of his regular twice-weekly rounds of golf at Doncaster Golf Club. When we meet at his home he is full of praise for Jordan Spieth – 60 years his junior – who triumphed at Royal Birkdale in the Open Championship less than 24 hours before.

Later on, the mental strength shown by Spieth will lead us to consider the importance of psychology in sport, particularly when we discuss two lost FA Cup semi-finals in the mid-1950s and last-day promotion near-misses of the early 1960s.

There are plenty of other subjects to talk about too, including a payments scandal, Sunderland's first-ever relegation, and a couple of former teammates who became two of the greatest footballing mavericks of the twentieth century – Len Shackleton and Brian Clough – with a man who made no fewer than a colossal 447 first-team appearances for the Red and Whites between 1952 and 1963.

When he was born, Stan's family were Sunderland through and through. He can't quite recall walking around his street in Horden in 1937 as a toddler with a large vase in his hands, pretending to be Sunderland skipper Raich Carter with the FA Cup following the 3-1 Wembley triumph over Preston North End, but his father proudly told him about it as he grew older.

And when the 15-year-old youngster signed amateur forms with the club in 1949, just a few months after the two of them had listened to radio reports of the shock 2-1 FA Cup fourth-round defeat on the slope at Yeovil Town with tears in their eyes, the story took on an extra resonance.

The 'Bank of England club' was famous throughout the country at that time and its biggest star was Shackleton, a true entertainer who was controversially only capped five times by England but was always a crowd favourite. Young Stan Anderson watched him in admiration regularly from the Roker Park terraces. 'My brother and I used to go to Sunderland all the time,' Stan remembers. 'He used to stand me in front of the railings and hold onto me by the shoulders so that I was safe. There were huge crowds in those days and when Sunderland were attacking you could often finish 20 yards down from where you started!'

As a boy Anderson played football whenever and wherever he could: at school and after school. He was selected to play for East Durham schoolboys and progressed into an England schoolboys' international. It seemed it was only going to be a matter of time before he could fulfil a childhood dream of becoming a professional footballer: 'People would say to me, "You're a good player, Stan" but I just kept on playing without thinking too much about it, to be honest. It was only when I was selected to play for England schoolboys that I thought to myself: "I could become a professional footballer." There were loads of lads in that side who went on to have professional careers, including Cliff Birkett, who was 16 when he got into the Manchester United side, and Dennis Viollet, who was another Busby Babe.

'My mother and father never went away on holiday,' remembers Stan, 'so the organised bus trips to watch me play for England schoolboys became their holidays. A lot of people from Horden went all over to watch me play. Just think about that: people from Horden, working in the mines, sitting on a bus and going all the way to places like Swansea to watch me play. From their point of view it was absolutely wonderful to go all the way down to Swansea.'

As well as becoming well-known in his home village, international recognition at schoolboy level was to bring instant attention from scouts up and down the country.

'It all happened very quickly,' Stan explains. 'I was 15 years of age and suddenly I started getting literally hundreds of letters from all sorts of places, including many First and Second Division clubs, coming through the door offering trials. It was fantastic, but my father soon stepped in. He told me, "You can put them all away, you're going to stay in the north-east so I can look after you."

'So I signed for Sunderland. It was a hard school. Tommy Irwin was our coach and the first thing he said to us was, "You lot think you can play, but you can't." There is a lot of luck involved in making it as a footballer. We had a nice lad with us called Albert Quinn. I'll never forget him; he was a really good inside-forward. One day, he jumped over this wire to get the ball and broke his leg. That was him finished. He wasn't re-signed.

'I got a job as a plumber with L.W. Evans, who was a director at the club, when I started. I used to have to get up at 5 o'clock in the morning to take a two-hour bus journey into Sunderland, with the same trip back at the end of the day. I lost count of the number of times I fell asleep on the bus going home and missed my stop. I did roofing: tiling and guttering. I got the so-called plumbers' professional licence, and I worked on the new baths in the dressing rooms at Roker Park! I was training part-time and Tommy Irwin was classed as the coach of the 'B' team, but you never saw him. He would come into the dressing room before a match and tell you what he wanted, but he never actually trained us.'

Anderson was given his first-team debut at the age of 18 in October 1952 in unpredictable circumstances. On arriving at Roker Park with his family after lunch to watch Sunderland play Portsmouth in the First Division, he was immediately summoned to manager Bill Murray's office upstairs. He was told that he was in the team at number four, due to both George Aitken and Willie Watson being unavailable to play. His astonished reply consisted of just one word: 'Today?' The match ended in a 1-1 draw. The attendance was 45,144. It was a big step up from what he was used to.

'I daren't say anything to anybody in the dressing room before the match,' Stan says. 'I thought people like Len Shackleton were "up there" compared to me. I just got my boots on as quickly as I could. I prayed that I wouldn't make a mistake. It was actually like that until I had played a few matches and the rest of the team realised that I could play a bit.

'Shack used to put his arm around me and say, "Stan, when you get the ball, look for me." And so that is what I did. I only had two options: Shack or Billy Bingham, who was out on the wing. I used to play it forward and then follow them from behind. That was satisfactory to them, because I was giving them the ball. It was totally expected that Shack would get more of the ball than anybody else.

'My main memory of that first match, other than the shock of playing, was the crowd,' Stan adds. 'The support for the club has always been remarkable. I don't care what anybody says, the Sunderland spectators – and I have stood as one of them – deserve their team to be in the top four of the Premier League every year.'

After breaking into the first team, the young Sunderland player's plumbing activities with L.W. Evans quickly went down to just one day a week. The rest of his time was spent training; not that he saw much in the way of a football.

'In those days you hardly ever practised with a ball,' Stan recalls. 'It was all about running and fitness training. We were actually told that we didn't need a ball to train with because apparently the more we didn't see a ball during the week, the more we would want it on a Saturday!

'So, Shack used to have to pinch one and hide it somewhere. Then he would round us all up for a game of head tennis in the gymnasium under the Roker End – until one of the coaching staff spotted us and then it was game over. It was daft. We were supposed to be professional footballers,' Stan gasps. 'Shack was a truly fantastic player, but he had the worst feet I have ever seen in my life. He was only 5 foot 7 something, but he had these huge feet. It's no wonder that he could bend the ball like he did. He could flick it up with his heel as well. Wonderful things like that. I would say he was the most talented player that I ever played with, in his dribbling ability and his passing ability. Also, his positional play was out of this world. He couldn't tackle to save his life – but he didn't have to.'

Within a year of making his first-team debut, Anderson became Sunderland's regular right-half, but it was the side's regular left-half, Arthur Wright, who inspired him to add those long diagonal passes to his natural game of strength and fitness.

'Arthur would ping these wonderful crosses,' Stan recalls. 'He had a brilliant left foot and he was the best long passer of the ball that I have ever seen. He could get it on the left-hand side and hit a 40-to-45-yard ball straight to Billy Bingham's feet. When I got into the team, I tried to replicate that – hitting the ball towards Tommy Reynolds on the other side. I was happy if I could hit one in three!'

Anderson was to be in the Sunderland side for the next 10 years. He even kept his place in the team during the length of his national service, which was spent at Catterick army camp 60 miles away.

'When I went into the army I did fear that I might be finished at Sunderland, but Bill Murray was shrewd in the respect that he always wanted me to go into national service at the age of 20, after I had established myself in the side, rather than go in at 18 and perhaps struggle to get into the side when I came out,' Stan says. 'He arranged for me to get a pass out every weekend, but the worst part of that was I got put on guard duty for some of the others' amusement, so I always had to get back to camp. In the end, I had to pay people to do my guard duty for me so that I could continue to play for Sunderland! I didn't enjoy guard duty, but I thoroughly enjoyed my time in the army. I made so many friends that I felt sad when it was time for me to leave and it occurred to me that I wasn't going to see these lads again.'

He has less happy memories of trying but failing to be reimbursed by Sunderland for the considerable expenses which mounted up while he was earning just 13s and 6d per week from national service with £1 per week from Sunderland to retain his services and a £6 match fee.

'Those guard-duty debts and my travel expenses totalled hundreds of pounds in the end,' Stan says. 'I told the Sunderland secretary, George Crow, about it and he always said the club would pay it back to me. But they never did. It was like getting blood out of a stone. He was the most miserable secretary I have ever met in my life! I got sick of asking in the end. They just wouldn't pay it. I was playing for Sunderland – travelling from Catterick and back every other weekend to do so – and I was actually losing money.'

This story is in stark contrast to the tarnished reputation Sunderland acquired at around this time due to events which were to rip the heart and soul out of the club, following a letter sent to the Football League in 1956, which was signed by a mysteriously named 'Mr Smith' and cited financial irregularities and undeclared payments to certain players at the club.

A Football League and Football Association inquiry later found that illicit payments had been made to Sunderland players totalling £5,247 14s 2d. The club was said to have paid contractors dealing in straw and tarmac excessive amounts of money, which were then returned as treasury notes and subsequently handed out to players as payments. Chairman Bill Ditchburn and director W.S. Martin were to be permanently suspended from any involvement in professional football, vice-chairman Stanley Ritson and L.W. Evans, who once employed Anderson as a plumber, were suspended *sine die*, and other directors were severely censured. The club was also fined £5,000 and ordered to pay full costs. Six players – four of whom were still at Sunderland – were later summoned to the FA to answer allegations. Five of them appeared but under advice did not answer any questions and were suspended *sine die*. They later admitted the charge and the suspensions were lifted, but each of them was made to forfeit their qualification for benefits.

Murray was fined £200 after the commission took into account that he had acted under instruction. After an association with the club as a player and a manager for nearly 30 years, he resigned. The days of the 'Bank of England club' were over.

'I was never interviewed, by the way,' Stan tells me. 'They went to see a lot of players, but they never came to see me. I was the local lad. I was the one player who was brought through and stayed in the side and that is still something special to me.

'But I do remember some of them playing cards on the coach going down to London and there was this wad of £5 notes. They would think nothing of losing 20 or 30 quid playing cards, which was a lot of money in those days. They would ask me why I wasn't playing and I would tell them, "I can't afford to play." I couldn't believe the money that was coming out of their pockets. I was thinking to myself, "Where the hell did they get this money from?" I just accepted it for what it was.'

Despite assembling the most attractive and expensive side in the country, Bill Murray failed to win silverware at Sunderland. His highest league finish was third in 1949-50, and the best FA Cup performances were back-to-back semi-finals in 1955 and 1956.

'To be honest, I don't know why we didn't achieve success,' Stan says. 'I think we should have won the first FA Cup semi-final we played, against Manchester City at Villa Park. Although whether the match should even have been played on such a badly waterlogged pitch is another matter. We were competent enough, but we lost a silly goal and couldn't get one back, and when you're chasing a game it's much more difficult than when you're winning.

'There was also the chance of a Sunderland versus Newcastle FA Cup final that year and everybody in the north-east was saying it would be absolutely brilliant if it happened, which of course it would have been. But it never materialised. They got there, we didn't. It was very disappointing and frustrating, really, particularly given the state of the pitch.

'We could have won the league as well. We lost to Chelsea immediately after the semi-final and they went on to win the title. So it obviously had an impact on us. We were never far away from the top of the table but we lost four league games in the month of March and we ended up finishing fourth.'

In the 1955-56 season Sunderland did play Newcastle in the FA Cup, visiting St James' Park at the quarter-final stage. The Magpies had won the trophy three times in the five previous seasons, but the Rokerites triumphed that day with two goals from Bill Holden.

'Newcastle were massive favourites to beat us, but they didn't play well,' Stan explains. 'At one stage Jimmy Scoular walked towards me and said, "I'll break your bloody legs if you come near me." How lovely of him – but that was the sort of thing that could happen in those days. Billy Elliott looked after him. He was the hard man in our side, a real character.'

Disappointingly, after knocking out the FA Cup holders, Sunderland were well-beaten 3-0 at Hillsborough in the semi-final by Birmingham City just a fortnight later.

'Personally, it was a great disappointment to lose in both of those semi-finals,' Stan admits. 'The FA Cup was *the* trophy to win. Shack used to say to us, "Bugger the league, we're going for the Cup."'

'We certainly didn't play well in either game,' Stan adds. 'The first one, we should have won. The second one, we were beaten quite easily. We couldn't score goals, and at the end of the day that is what it's all about. It got to the point where I felt desperate to win something, but I don't know if everybody had the same feeling as I did.'

Bill Murray's 11th full season as manager at Roker Park was to be his last. It was a sorrowful campaign, which resulted in Sunderland finishing in their lowest-ever league position of 20th in the First Division, avoiding relegation by just one place. But it is also indisputable that events on the pitch had been seriously affected by events off the pitch.

Murray resigned in the summer of 1957. His replacement was to be the tough taskmaster Alan Brown. A Sunderland fan in his youth, Brown, who was nicknamed 'the Bomber', was all about hard work and fitness training.

But he had also built an admirable reputation at Burnley for a successful youth policy. This had helped take them to seventh in the First Division the previous season. Furthermore, many of the youngsters that he nurtured during his time there – including Jimmy Adamson and Jimmy McIlroy – went on to bring the First Division title to Turf Moor just three years later.

However, after the first match of the 1957-58 season with Sunderland – a 1-0 defeat at Arsenal – the Bomber was to be without his star player.

'I am sure that the reason why Len Shackleton retired from football after just one game playing under Alan Brown was that he thought he was going to be required to have to run miles and miles and miles in training every day and he wasn't prepared to do that,' Stan says. 'There was never any injury, I don't care what people say. Len was as fit as a fiddle the day it happened. He played one match under Browny and by the Monday he had retired from the game.

'The manager's whole attitude was about fitness. Keeping fit was easy because we always started off with six laps around the track and we did a lot of running up to Seaburn and back again, which would be a distance of well over six miles. It was all to do with physical exercise with him. There was no ball work again. I remember George Whitelaw, who came down from Scotland, once went to pick a ball up and Browny shouted at him: "Leave that bloody ball alone." He was another one. He just wouldn't let us have the ball! "You don't need the ball," he would boom. So, we never practised. In fact, I spent more time practising in the army than I did at Sunderland.

'I admit we were a fit side,' Stan adds. 'But on a personal note I didn't get on well with Browny. He only made me captain due to an injury to Charlie Hurley, who told me I might as well carry on. I didn't like the bloke when it came to tactics. He probably didn't like my style of play. That's fine, I can accept that.

'From a mental strength point of view, he was very, very strong. What he thought was right was always going to be right in his eyes. He would stick rigidly to his guns. Nobody could change his mind.'

During his first season in charge at Roker Park Brown regularly tried to replace experienced players with youngsters, and the results were often disastrous. Within the first few months of the campaign, the Red and Whites had suffered many heavy defeats including successive 7-0 and 6-0 thrashings at Blackpool and Burnley respectively in new signing Charlie Hurley's first two matches with his new club in October 1957. With eight matches to go Sunderland were bottom of the table and, after 68 unbroken years in the First Division, the fear of relegation was hovering bleakly over Roker Park like never before.

'I went in to see Browny at that time and I was quite honest with him,' Stan recalls. 'I said to him, "You can leave me out if you like but you're going to have to stick another youngster in my place and we have already got four youngsters in the side and we're fighting a relegation battle here." I felt it was putting too much pressure on the younger players when we had experienced men being held back in the reserves, and I told him so.

'His reply to me was short: "That's your opinion, is it?" When I said it was, he just said, "Well, it's wrong." You would never even get an "I'll think about it" from him. It was always, "No." He domineered players to the point where everybody was frightened of him, and players should not be frightened of their manager. Some of them used to call him names behind his back and some of them used to avoid him if they could. It was ridiculous. Anyhow, by the end of the season, we were relegated.

'It's no use me criticising Alan Brown all these years on because obviously other people have different opinions about him,' Stan adds. 'But I don't believe you can get youngsters to fight a relegation battle. It's too hard for them. There were no easy games for us, they were always pressure games. You can expect experienced players to survive that, but you can't expect youngsters to do so. He should have gone for experience in my opinion, but he didn't.'

Worse was to come. Sunderland's first season in the Second Division ended in 15th place. The following campaign ended with a final position of 16th. Moreover, players and supporters were now getting used to a different type of opponent in different types of environment, often in front of crowds of under 10,000.

'It was a terrible time,' Stan remembers. 'We were such a big club that the opposition would do anything to beat us. Second Division football wasn't football as I knew it either; it was kicking and tackling and heavy stuff. I lasted about one-and-a-half seconds in one match against Walsall at home before I was carried off. We had some real battles in the Second Division, but we just had to accept it.'

In January 1961 the maximum wage was abolished, and Fulham and England captain Johnny Haynes became the first player to earn £100 per week. At Sunderland the wages were not as high as that.

'Len Ashurst was the one person I would listen to more than anybody else at Sunderland,' Stan says. 'We would sit on the train together and he would say to me, "We should be getting more money, you know, Stan." He always used to talk about the size of the attendances – 50,000 or more – and then question why we were only on £14 a week!

'You would think that the money coming into the club far outweighed what they were paying the players,' Stan adds. 'So when the maximum wage was abolished, it was obviously great news. I remember Charlie Hurley and I got together and we decided to ask the club to double our wages, from something like £20 at the time to £40. Charlie went in and I always had a feeling he asked for a bit more. Anyway, I went in and I finished up with £32 a week. I didn't want to sign for that, but I did in the end. They still took us to the cleaners, and I think they knew that.'

After three seasons out of the national spotlight, Brown began to develop a team and a strategy that would eventually reap rewards. During the 1960-61 season Sunderland knocked Arsenal out of the FA Cup and came close to preventing Tottenham Hotspur from becoming the first team in the twentieth century to win the Double.

'I would say that the proudest day I ever had with Sunderland – well, the one that stands out in my mind – would be when we knocked Arsenal out of the FA Cup,' Stan says. 'It was a huge thing for me because I was having problems with the manager and I scored the two goals that beat Arsenal that day, and they were a top-class club. There was a funny moment afterwards when the chairman, Syd Collings, came into the dressing room and said to me, "Well played, Stan, that was a good goal you scored." Well, when I told him that I'd got both of them, he just said, "Did you?" He didn't even know I had scored the winning goal! That was bloody typical: my big day and the chairman doesn't even know what I have actually done.'

Sunderland progressed in the competition with victories over Bill Shankly's Liverpool and Norwich City before being drawn at home to First Division champions-elect Tottenham in the quarter-finals. A crowd of 61,326 turned up to see it and more than a few of them were on the pitch when 18-year-old Willie McPheat equalised for Sunderland in the second half. Spurs captain Danny Blanchflower later said that the Roker

Roar celebrating that goal was the loudest noise he ever heard during his entire career.

'We should have beaten Tottenham at Sunderland and knocked them out,' Stan says. 'One thing I will always remember from that match is getting the ball from the right-hand side and John Dillon, who was a right-footed player, coming inside from the left wing. I played this perfect ball straight to him from 40 yards and I saw a Tottenham defender coming towards him, mistakenly thinking that he was left-footed. I was sure John was going to score. He was a good striker of the ball with his right foot and he had space. He didn't even get a shot in! I couldn't believe it. John probably had our best chance to win it later in the match as well, but Bill Brown made a good save. We were all over them. Danny Blanchflower came off the pitch at the end. We shook hands and he said to me, "We've been a bit lucky today, Stan, haven't we?"'

Sunderland succumbed 5-0 at White Hart Lane in the replay and Tottenham went on to win the Double.

Buoyed by this quarter-final appearance in the FA Cup and a sixth-placed finish in the Second Division, Sunderland supporters were further excited when Alan Brown pulled off the summer signing of one of the most prolific goalscorers in the country, Brian Clough, aged 26, who had amassed a total of 197 goals in 213 matches for Middlesbrough.

Clough was an instant success at Sunderland, scoring 29 times in 34 league games as Brown's side sustained a promotion push until the final day of the 1961-62 season at Swansea Town. A win would have sent the club back up to the First Division. Clough gave them the lead and Anderson forced a great save from Johnny King, but the match finished in a 1-1 draw and Leyton Orient were promoted alongside Second Division champions Liverpool.

There was to be some consolation for Anderson when he received a call-up to the full England squad for the first time towards the end of that season.

'Personally, I had a season which was as good as I ever had and it was fantastic that I won my first full international cap for England against Austria at Wembley in April 1962,' Stan says. 'But by that time I was 29 years old and the likes of Nobby Stiles and Bobby Moore were coming through, so it was never going to develop for me. I had been sent off in an Under-23 match in Bulgaria for retaliating after being spat at, and that stopped my development with England because I was the first player ever to be sent off while playing for the national side. That was held against me for years, and I didn't get picked for anything as a result.

'I did play against Scotland after the Austria match, which was great,' Stan adds. 'That was my wish. I always wanted to play against them. That was the big match in those days and it was a lovely experience, even though we lost 2-0.'

Anderson was selected to go to the 1962 World Cup in Chile. Given squad number 14, he was the last Sunderland player to go to a World Cup with England. He didn't play, but he was grateful to learn a footballing lesson from the brilliant Brazilians, Garrincha and all, in the 3-1 quarter-final defeat in Viña del Mar.

'I was in the stands for that match and I was left wondering at the end why we didn't play like they did,' Stan says. 'It wasn't necessarily the fact that they had great players, it was more the fact that when they got the ball they didn't give it away. They would keep the ball, move it around and create chances for themselves, and they usually finished every move with a shot on goal. We were in the game just as much as they were – but they beat us 3-1. I have always had the opinion that we tend to give the ball away too much, and that if we could only use our strength and work-rate to the point where we could develop the passing and movement of teams like Holland and Italy we would be a much better team.'

The 1962-63 season was to provide a similar scenario for Sunderland. Positioned top of the table at the start of the final day, they played third-placed Chelsea at home, requiring just a draw to go up. They lost 1-0 and finished third again, this time behind Stoke City and Tommy Docherty's side.

'I often wonder why we never got promotion in those years because we were regularly in the top six – even the top three – in the early 1960s, but we never quite made it,' Stan ponders. 'Maybe it was a bit of mind over matter? I don't know. Look at Jordan Spieth in the Open yesterday. He was having such a terrible time where he lost a three-stroke overnight lead and even went one down to his opponent. Then, just as I thought he has gone, he goes birdie, eagle, birdie, birdie and all of a sudden he is three shots ahead again. He wanted it that badly. You could see it in the expression on his face. He willed himself to win it.

'I always used to go out to play and think we could win,' Stan adds. 'It didn't always work out that way, but if there are doubts anywhere, it can have an effect. We played Swansea and Chelsea on the last days of those seasons with promotion there for the taking for us, but we didn't manage it, and I don't know why.'

However, without a cruel injury suffered by Clough on Boxing Day 1962, it is likely that the Rokerites would have been crowned champions long before that final day slip up against Chelsea. The popular centre-forward had contributed another stunning strike record of 24 goals in 24 league games that season when a collision with Bury goalkeeper Chris Harker at the Roker End effectively ended his career.

'When I think of the tragic circumstances, it was such a great shame for Cloughie,' Stan says. 'I was in the stands that day and it was a sickening thing to see, although it was a pure accident. I remember going to see Brian in hospital and he told me, "I'll be fit" but people were saying it was a really bad break, and it turned out to be so because he was never going to be at the standard that he was before, it was just impossible. I think he could have played 50 times or more for England.

'I would watch Cloughie and try to work out just how he managed to get into these positions all the time where the ball would come off a defender and he would be in the right place to knock it in. He was an absolutely fantastic player. His mind seemed to be a yard ahead of everybody else's.'

Sunderland were without Clough but promotion was finally achieved the following season, helped by a 39-goal partnership in the league from Johnny Crossan and Nic Sharkey. However, the captain of the last few years was no longer around to celebrate, after making his final appearance against Cardiff City in a 3-3 draw in September 1963. Two days later Brown explained to him that Martin Harvey would play at right-half at Plymouth Argyle in midweek. Within a few weeks, Anderson left Roker Park.

'Browny still made me travel all the way from Sunderland down to Plymouth for that match,' Stan says. 'He dropped me, but he still made me travel. I asked him, "You don't need me to go all the way down to Plymouth, do you?" and he just said, "You'll travel." That was nice of him, wasn't it? That was typical of the man. He was never going to play me, and I never played for Sunderland again. Martin Harvey was the regular right-half from then onwards.'

'A few weeks later he [Brown] came to visit me at home. He told me there was a club interested in signing me. After about 45 minutes he eventually told me that the club in question was Newcastle United and their manager was sitting outside in his car.

'I couldn't believe it. I said to him, "You are telling me that you have got Joe Harvey in the car? And you have waited three-quarters-of-an-hour to do so? I am a friend of his: bring him in." I knew Joe well. I used to play golf with him and Bob Stokoe. The two of them were the best of friends, but on the golf course it could be a very different story. I remember once Joe was in a bunker and he touched the sand with his practice swing, and Bob shouted out to him, "Two-shot penalty." And so it went on. "I'm bloody telling you," Bob said, pointing his finger at him. It was only supposed to be a friendly round of golf, but that is just how they were. Afterwards, it was all fine, of course.

'Anyhow, Joe came inside the house and I told him there was no way that I could sign for Newcastle as all my relations were Sunderland supporters. I knew for a fact that my father would go berserk if I did. Joe still asked me to go and see him the next day. I said I would, but I also repeated that I wouldn't ever sign for Newcastle.

'I went up there and I signed! I had the change of heart because I was sick of Browny. I would have loved to have stayed at Sunderland for all of my career, but it didn't work out like that. I rang my father up and he didn't speak to me for three weeks! He said he would never go and watch me play for them, but he did . . . eventually.'

Anderson won promotion back into the First Division with Newcastle the following season. He later played for Middlesbrough as well, before starting his managerial career at Ayresome Park. He also managed AEK Athens, Queens Park Rangers, Doncaster Rovers and Bolton Wanderers.

In late 1978 he received an invitation from his old friend Brain Clough to attend the European Cup tie between Nottingham Forest and AEK Athens at the City Ground.

'I was interested to have a look at my old team and see how they had developed in the five years or so since I left. Forest won 5-1 and as Brian came over to have a word with me in the boardroom afterwards he heard this steward mutter, "Forest will never have an easier game than that." Well, he went for this bloke, calling him disrespectful and threatening him with the sack and all sorts,' Stan laughs.

Forest went on to win the European Cup that season. Their left-back was Frank Clark, who almost signed for Anderson at Doncaster before Clough intervened with a better offer.

Anderson retired from management in 1981 at the age of 47. To this day he remains the only man to have captained Sunderland, Newcastle and Middlesbrough to this day.

5

John MacPhail had been a solid centre-half in the Scottish Premier League and the Football League for many years when, in the latter part of his career, his former York City manager Denis Smith provided him with the opportunity to sample the Roker Roar.

Sunderland were good for MacPhail but, equally, he was also good for Sunderland. Arriving at the lowest point in the club's history, just as they had been relegated to the Third Division, MacPhail was a key member of the team that won two promotions in three seasons.

He signed off for Sunderland by playing in the club's first match back in the First Division in August 1990; his solitary top-flight appearance in England in a career full of bumps, bruises and boisterousness.

JOHN MacPHAIL

MEETS LANCE HARDY

It was the best of times, it was the worst of times . . . Sunderland, 1987: a tale of two seasons.

The prologue is set in the summer of 1985 – just a few months after Sunderland played in the League Cup final at Wembley – with the arrival of Lawrie McMenemy following the club's relegation to the Second Division after five seasons in the top flight.

McMenemy was seen as a glorious appointment at the time. He was heralded as the new Messiah as he was greeted by thousands of Sunderland supporters at Roker Park. Ironically, he was to be replaced by the old Messiah less than two years later when Bob Stokoe had to return to the club in a caretaker-manager role in a desperate last-ditch attempt to try to prevent an unthinkable relegation to the Third Division.

McMenemy had tried to repeat a method that had worked so well for him at Southampton, by bringing in experienced First Division players such as George Burley, Eric Gates, Frank Gray, Alan Kennedy and David Swindlehurst. The aim was instant promotion. 'This club could be one of the biggest in the country,' Big Mac told *Football Focus* early that season. Five defeats in the first five games with no goals scored underlined the task in hand. Relegation was only averted on the last day of the 1985-86 season and the situation did not improve during the following campaign. After a 2-1 home defeat by Sheffield United – the fifth in six matches – in front of just 8,544 fans (the lowest home league crowd at Roker Park since the days of midweek afternoon kick-offs during the three-day week in 1974) calls came for McMenemy's head amidst reports of criminal damage to his car. The highest-earning manager in English football at the time resigned shortly afterwards.

Stokoe was a passionate and popular temporary replacement. He came out of retirement – trilby still intact – with his heart on his sleeve to try to keep Sunderland in the Second Division. The last few matches of the 1986-87 season were not without drama, but sadly the Rokerites were relegated following a two-legged play-off semi-final defeat by Gillingham. The away leg was lost 3-2, the home leg was won 4-3 after extra time, the aggregate score was 6-6. Therefore, Sunderland became the first and remain the only English league side ever to be relegated on the away goals rule.

Third Division football beckoned as the pits and shipyards were closed down in and around Sunderland. Stokoe left the club he loved and was never to manage again. It was a bleak time . . .

Sunderland chairman Bob Murray decided that the task of resuscitating this once great club should fall to the York City management duo of Denis Smith and Viv Busby, who had taken the Minstermen to two FA Cup fifth-round replays against Liverpool in successive seasons in the mid-1980s. They had also knocked McMenemy's Sunderland out of the League Cup.

Smith was not able to splash the cash in the same way that McMenemy had done just two seasons earlier. Instead, he began his Roker reign by shrewdly investing in two defenders – both of whom were full of determination, heart and spirit. One was right-back John Kay, from Wimbledon, and the other was the Dundee-born centre-half John MacPhail, aged 31 at the time and supposedly heading into the twilight of his career at Bristol City. Both proved to be inspired signings. Both were ever-presents in the Third Division campaign.

Thirty years on, MacPhail is now a sales executive with Skoda in the north-east. He fondly remembers the day he signed for Sunderland. Touchingly, he views it as one of the highlights of his 24-year career in football.

'I played for Denis Smith at York,' John recalls. 'We had some great times there, with FA Cup matches against Arsenal and Liverpool, but the two of us had fallen out badly after I had asked him for a new contract and a £50 pay rise!

'I moved on to Bristol City, played at Wembley for them in the Freight Rover Trophy, and towards the end of that season I became aware that Denis was starting to show an interest in taking me back to York. My wife is from York, so obviously that would have worked out very well. Five days later, Denis gets the Sunderland job! I thought that was that. I presumed I would see out my time at Bristol. Pre-season, I was doing some weights when Denis called Terry Cooper, the Bristol City manager, and they did a deal for me there and then. I signed for £23,000.

'I lived in Weston-super-Mare,' John adds. 'Denis told me to get the first train up to the north-east. I had to change trains and all sorts and got up there for about 6 p.m. When I went to Roker Park it was just wonderful. I had never been there before and I thought it was absolutely fantastic, a lovely stadium. I met Denis and Bob Murray. The deal was done quickly. It was fairy tale stuff, really.'

If signing for Sunderland was a fairytale for MacPhail, so too had been his professional debut for Dundee at Ibrox Park against Rangers, the team he supported as a boy, back in 1975.

'I was a centre-half and centre-halves in those days were very physical people, kicking and all that,' John says. 'The Dundee manager, David White, would never try me in the first team because I would get booked every week playing for the reserves. In fact, I got sent off twice in five days at one time, just before I was selected for the first team. We played Partick Thistle at Dens Park in a semi-final and their centre-forward tackled me waist-high with his boots, so I just headbutted him, knocked him out and got sent off, obviously. That was on the Tuesday, the following Saturday we played Dumbarton at Boghead Park and there was a mêlée in the middle of the park. I went to kick the ball, but I kicked this guy's head instead. I didn't mean it, but I got sent off again. So, the manager felt that he couldn't trust me.

'There were only about eight weeks of the season to go and I felt I now had nothing to lose – I was heading for a free transfer because he had never tried me and I didn't think he ever would. I was sitting in the physio's room with a bit of a dead leg one day and, as the manager walked in, I started cussing and swearing: "Give me one chance and I won't let you down. I promise," I told him.

'He walked out the room and then the phone went and I was asked to go through and see him,' John adds. 'I thought I was going to get my P45 there and then. But, instead, he said to me, "Will you be fit for Saturday?" I said, "Yes" – we were only playing against Rangers at Ibrox by the way!

'After training, we all used to run into the changing room at Dundee because the team for Saturday would be put up on the wall. This time, I was down as the 16th man. Wow! I thought I had made it. Whether I played or not, it didn't matter, I was going to be at Ibrox with 45,000 to 50,000 people there, playing against legends like John Greig, Alex MacDonald, Derek Johnstone, Derek Parlane. These players were superstars – I had pictures of them on my walls at home.

'I was named as sub and just sitting on the bench, watching the match, as we were getting beaten 2-0 after only about 20 minutes when Alex Caldwell, our centre-half, pulled his hamstring and the manager says, "John, get yourself ready, you're on." I went, "You're f***ing joking?" I was bricking myself, but once you cross the white line, you're on your own. I played very well. I got man of the match in the Sunday papers, and I was given a score of nine out of ten. I remember one moment when a corner kick came in, I was in the six-yard box and I chested it and laid it back to the goalkeeper. I didn't let them down. We got beat 3-0, but what an occasion!

'On the Tuesday we played against Motherwell, who had Willie Pettigrew, a terrific player, in their side. I was a man-to-man marker in those days and I was told to mark him. We beat them 1-0 and the big headline in the *Dundee Courier* was: "Gentle Giant Tames Pettigrew". The boss trusted me from then onwards. That is when my career took off. David White was the man who gave me a chance and I really appreciated that. I thanked him for it. But it really came down to me feeling that I had nothing to lose and having a pop at him that day. I got a new contract and stayed there for a few more seasons.

'Gordon Strachan was in the team with me at Dundee,' John adds. 'He was like the next Alan Ball. He even came onto the pitch in white boots, just like Alan Ball. Gordon was a fantastic player, a passionate guy and a winner. He always will be a winner. Those were great days with some great players: Gordon, Jocky Scott, George Stewart, Gordon Wallace, Duncan Lambie, John Duncan . . .

'Some time later, Tommy Gemmell, the old Celtic player, took over. We had played together at Dundee and we didn't get on particularly well. One of the scouts from down south had watched me and it led to me coming down to England and joining Sheffield United. When I was transferred, the manager put in his notes, "John's type of game is suited for English football rather than Scottish football." I thought to myself, "How does he know anything about English football? He's been up in Scotland most of his life!" It was just an excuse, I think.

'So, I left Dundee at the age of 22 to join Sheffield United and it was to be the best five years of my life. I played with some fantastic players and I made some fantastic friends, some of whom I am still friends with to this day.'

One of MacPhail's new teammates was the flamboyant Argentinian midfielder Alex Sabella, who played a starring role in the Blades' 3-2 win over Sunderland at Bramall Lane in October 1978 in front of the *Match of the Day* cameras. I was there that day, aged 10, and he was mesmeric.

'When people ask me who was the best player I played against, I always say it was probably Kenny Dalglish, when York played Liverpool in the FA Cup. When people ask me who was the best player I played with, I always say Alex Sabella. He was absolutely brilliant and two paces ahead of anybody else,' John says. 'The story goes that Danny Bergara, Sheffield United's Uruguayan coach and the most passionate man I have ever seen in my life, went over to Argentina to watch two players. One was for sale at £100,000 and one was for sale at £300,000. They could only afford £100,000 and that got them Sabella. The other player was Diego Maradona!

'Alex was all left peg, just like Diego Maradona,' John adds. 'He was as good as Maradona as well as far as I am concerned. He had a cultured left foot and he knew exactly what he was doing. I once watched him score in a practice match against the reserves and he beat seven men. The last man was the goalkeeper and Alex went to hit it and just put his foot on it and rolled it in after the goalkeeper had dived. I had never seen anything like that in my life. I just stood and applauded. He was an absolute genius as a player.'

As a manager, Sabella wasn't too bad either. In 2014 he guided Argentina to the World Cup final in Rio de Janeiro, where they lost 1-0 to Germany after extra time.

'I really hoped he would win it,' John says. 'He was just a terrific talent and a great guy. Admittedly, sometimes he didn't fancy playing in away matches at Plymouth and places like that, but he could get away with it because he was that big a name at the club and you couldn't touch him.

'The two of us could have made history and joined Leeds United in the first million-pound deal,' John adds. 'I was playing well and Alex was playing well and the Leeds manager Jimmy Adamson apparently put a million-pound bid in for the two of us, but the club quashed it. A year later Derby County came in for me with a £100,000 bid. I heard about it on the radio just after I had finished a round of golf!'

Despite interest from elsewhere, MacPhail remained at Bramall Lane and won a Fourth Division championship medal under Sunderland's 1973 FA Cup final goalscoring hero Ian Porterfield. He left in 1983 when he signed for York City.

'Me and Ian Porterfield never got on,' John says. 'Two Jocks clashing, possibly – we just didn't click. It was one of those things: he was affecting me and I was affecting him. So something had to give. But, as a coach, he was one of the best I have ever seen.

'Denis Smith came in for me and I signed for York,' John adds. 'I always classed myself as an ordinary player, but I always had a big heart. That was probably why I lasted in football for so long when a lot of people who were maybe better than me did not have half of that. I always gave 110 per cent and I have always been like that. Denis wrote a very nice line about me in his book, something about having 11 John MacPhails in his side . . . that for me is just the pinnacle.'

MacPhail won another Fourth Division championship medal with York, but it was two back-to-back FA Cup runs that gripped the nation, including a 1-0 fourth-round win over Arsenal at Bootham Crescent and two 1-1 draws in the fifth round against Liverpool. MacPhail was partnered by future Sunderland manager Ricky Sbragia in central defence at that time.

'Those cup matches were fantastic times,' John adds. 'Me and Ricky Sbragia at the back. That's where the club got its money for the new stands, hospitality, new showers and things like that. Yet they couldn't find an extra £50 for me!

'I really admired Denis, but he lost my respect over that. I wanted to stay at York, but it wasn't to be. It went to a tribunal. Denis was there, Terry Cooper was there, Bert Millichip, the FA chairman, was there, Brendon Batson of the PFA was there. Denis said he valued me at £60,000. The tribunal decided the fee should be £13,500. Denis erupted. He walked out. He wouldn't even allow me to go back to York to pick up my boots!

'I enjoyed my brief time at Bristol City. I played alongside David Moyes at the back and we got to Wembley in the Freight Rover Trophy final, where we lost on penalties [to Mansfield Town]. Then came my move to Sunderland. I thought there were a few prima donnas there. That was my opinion. I knew they had got relegated and Denis Smith had gone in with Viv Busby. There were some great players there: Gary Bennett, Eric Gates, Mark Proctor and so on. But it was a rebuilding job now. The players just needed the best bringing out of them, and Denis and Viv got the best out of them. They did that for eight or nine months straight. Everybody did their job. If you do your job, you get rewarded, and our reward was promotion.

'I had never heard the Roker Roar before I got up there. The first time I heard it was the evening home match against Mansfield Town on August Bank Holiday Monday. It was just incredible. I could feel the hair on the back of my neck. I got goose pimples running out to that.

'Me and Benno had a little bet before the season started about which one of us would score the most goals. He was a bit of a goalscorer, supposedly!' John laughs. 'He offered to bet me £25 that he would score more goals than me. I took it, I won the bet – and I am still waiting for my money! We always rib one another with regards to that to this day. To be fair, I didn't tell him that I was going to be taking the penalty kicks!

'I had taken penalties previously at York and I scored a few there. Penalties are all about confidence, really. You just put the ball down and hit it,' John says. 'I was quite fortunate during my first season at Sunderland. I scored 16 goals – 11 were penalty kicks and five were headers.'

The first two of MacPhail's 11 successful penalties that season came in the 4-1 win over Mansfield. They helped to put Sunderland top of the table after three wins and a draw from the opening four games. But then the momentum slowed. Three successive draws and two defeats, including a 2-0 loss at home to Chester City, left the Rokerites in 12th place at the end of September.

Mark Proctor was sold to First Division Sheffield Wednesday for £275,000, and £80,000 of the fee was spent on a 19-year-old striker from York who had once cleaned MacPhail's boots.

Marco Gabbiadini's impact was almost immediate. After making his debut against Chester, he netted two goals in three successive wins against Fulham, Aldershot and Wigan Athletic. By the time Sunderland went to Blackpool in mid-October they were top of the league again.

'That was a great away day,' MacPhail recalls. 'I got both our goals at Blackpool in a 2-0 win, one was a header and one was a penalty. It was party time for the Sunderland fans that weekend. There was a party atmosphere at a lot of the away matches that season. The fans had the confidence that their team was going to perform and everybody was up for it.'

Sunderland remained in the promotion places from October until the end of the season. The Third Division championship was secured in a 1-0 win at Port Vale at the end of April.

'The Port Vale game was very important,' John says. 'We couldn't lose, we knew that. We didn't played that great, we didn't play that badly. We had a job to do and we did it. We won 1-0 with a goal from Gatesy.

'Every time we went out we had this confidence that we would win,' John adds. 'That's what we had under Denis and Viv at that time. The players have to take the biggest accolade, really, because we were consistent all season. It was a marathon not a sprint: 46 games over nine months. Denis and Viv got it spot on.'

The party continued with two more wins over Northampton Town and Rotherham United. MacPhail scored penalties in both of them, even though he had to wait his turn after a fan had run on to the pitch at Millmoor and taken the spot kick for him!

'That was very funny,' John remembers. 'They were great days. We had a good team, a blend of exciting young players and experience, and when you start winning games your confidence just grows and grows. Everybody played together and pulled together and that is what you need to succeed. Viv Busby was a big instigator of that camaraderie among the players, because he was a players' man himself. Viv was always there to put his arm around you. Denis, the hard man that he is, would do the same sometimes. He would also knock you down if you needed it. He would tell you in no uncertain terms. But all the players adhered to that. We played for the shirt. I think the days of playing for the shirt have gone. Nowadays it is about money. How do you motivate a millionaire? You can't do it. Players seem to have egos these days. In our day it was all about heart and passion.'

Gabbiadini and Gates got 40 league goals between them in the 1987-88 season. The G-Force was well and truly established. MacPhail was the third top scorer. He comfortably won his bet with Bennett.

'Marco was a godsend to us,' John says. 'He just had something that nobody else had. He was great at nutmegging people and he had tremendous pace as well. Along with Eric, the two of them were brilliant. Eric would put the balls through and Marco had the pace to chase and the ability to score goals. Eric got more than a few as well, including the important one at Port Vale. It was just a phenomenal partnership.

'We also had good young players coming through, like Gordon Armstrong and Gary Owers. Denis Smith brought in John Kay. What a great, tenacious player he was, and another one who always gave 110 per cent. And that is what you needed in the Third Division. Denis knew I knew that division. That is probably the reason why he bought me.

'Nobody had ever heard of me in Sunderland when I signed,' John adds. 'So the greatest accolade for me was when I came second to Paul Gascogine in the North-East Sports Writers Player of the Year award in 1988. That was a great honour for me, and something I didn't know anything about. Denis Smith and Viv Busby kept it quiet. All the dickie bows were over there and so I got mortal. All of a sudden, compère Roger Tames is saying: "In second place: John MacPhail of Sunderland!" You should have seen me trying to get up on that stage!'

The good times were beginning to come back. The attendance of 29,454 for the last home match of the season against Northampton Town was the biggest league crowd at Roker Park in five years, since the visit of Manchester United in the First Division.

The 1988-89 season was one of consolidation for Sunderland. They finished 11th. But slowly and surely Denis Smith had added to his squad, signing Welsh international winger Colin Pascoe, highly rated Welsh international goalkeeper Tony Norman, German striker Thomas Hauser, and left-back Paul Hardyman.

'Thomas is a lovely guy,' John says. 'I remember when he came to Sunderland on trial and he scored four goals in a practice match. He hit one from about 30 yards into the top corner, and he met a corner kick on the penalty spot with a header which went straight into the corner as well. I had never seen goals like it in my life. We were all asking, "Who is this guy?" He was never the same again! Obviously, they took a gamble on him and he just wasn't good enough for that level. Although he got a few goals for us [11 over four seasons], he never emulated what he did in that training session. It was a one-off.'

The popular return of former Sunderland and England midfielder Paul Bracewell to Roker Park early in the 1989-90 season was to be another significant signing. There was to be another promotion charge. It was to be achieved in extraordinary circumstances.

Meanwhile, Hardyman immediately took over penalty-taking duties. 'I was fine with that,' John says. 'Paul was a good penalty-taker. I had missed one at Leeds in the previous season and the goal was getting smaller and smaller!' MacPhail still notched some vital goals, including a late equaliser at Blackburn Rovers in September and the only goal of the game at home to Bradford City in October.

Up to Halloween night in 1989 MacPhail had been an almost ever-present for Denis Smith's side, missing just one league game and one Simod Cup match in nearly two-and-a-half seasons for Sunderland. That was all to change when he suffered a fractured cheekbone after he was elbowed in the face against Barnsley in a midweek encounter at Roker Park. He was to be out of action until the New Year.

'I was quite fortunate with injuries over the years,' MacPhail recalls. 'But I did smash both my cheekbones. One was done by Kerry Dixon, of Chelsea, when I was playing for Sheffield

United, and the other was done by Ian Banks, of Barnsley, when I was at Sunderland. I still have no feeling in parts of my face due to those injuries, because when you sever the nerve below the eye it takes part of the feeling away. The operation involves drilling a hole in your head and having an iron rod fitted to put the bone in place again. I smashed one of my cheekbones in four bits and the other one in three.'

When MacPhail returned from injury Sunderland were positioned in the play-off places, behind Leeds United, Sheffield United and Newcastle United. There were some big guns in the Second Division that season and they were all firing. But after Leeds defeated Sunderland 1-0 at Roker Park in March, The Lads were down to 10th in the table. Any hopes of promotion looked like being put on hold.

Denis Smith then played his joker, unleashing the exciting young winger Kieron Brady at home against West Ham United. Sunderland won 4-3, Brady scored with an overhead kick, was voted man of the match, and received a glowing thumbs up from one of his opponents that day, Liam Brady, who had won major honours in a glittering career with the likes of Arsenal and Juventus.

Brady kept his place in the Sunderland side and simply dazzled in successive away victories at Bradford City and Sheffield United. Soon Sunderland were up to fifth. They finished the season in sixth and reached the play-offs. But, by then, with just nine starts to his name that season, Brady was out of favour and out of the team.

'Kieron was a great player,' John remembers. 'He had so much talent. He could have been the next George Best with the skill he had. He had everything. He played some great games for Sunderland. But it just got wasted. I remember he was living with [youth coach] Malcolm Crosby at the hostel and he was always sneaking out, going drinking. Crozza caught him a few

times but he couldn't really do anything about it. At that age –
18 or so – you have got to be so dedicated to be the best and
I don't think Kieron had that in him, to be honest. But what a
player! It is sad that his talent was wasted. It quickly went from
something to nothing.'

Leeds and Sheffield United won automatic promotion.
Sunderland, finishing sixth, were to play their arch-rivals, third-
placed Newcastle United, in the play-offs over two legs. The
winners would meet either Swindon Town or Blackburn Rovers
at Wembley for a place in the First Division.

Both north-east derby matches during the regular 1989-90
season were tight affairs and both ended in draws. The first leg
of the play-off semi-final was to be no different, although that
doesn't quite tell the whole story . . .

In injury time at Roker Park, with the score locked at 0-0,
Mark Stimson fouled Marco Gabbiadini in the penalty box in
front of a vociferous Fulwell End. Paul Hardyman was given
the task of giving Sunderland the lead from the penalty spot. He
had scored four penalties that season, but this effort was tame
and Newcastle goalkeeper John Burridge comfortably dived to
his right to make a save. As he smothered the ball, Hardyman
followed through in the hope of getting there first. It appeared
that contact was made between his boot and Burridge's head.
The Newcastle players frantically appealed to the referee, Vic
Callow, and Hardyman was sent off, ruling himself out of the
second leg and any possible play-off final at Wembley should
it follow. Furthermore, the odds of Sunderland getting to the
twin towers seemed to have gone with him . . .

'Paul never touched him,' John says adamantly all these
years later. 'I spoke to Budgie about it afterwards. He told me
that he never touched him. I admit it looks like he did, but he
didn't. I think the sending-off was all to do with the reaction by
the Newcastle players.

'So, we draw 0-0 at home, miss a penalty, get a man sent off, and we are without him at their place. We were expected to get beat heavily. Nobody gave us a chance. Everybody expected a landslide. But come Wednesday night it was hallelujah.

'It was a script, wasn't it? Newcastle had some great players and two prolific goalscorers in Mark McGhee and Micky Quinn. But that all goes out of the window with derby games. That's where the passion comes in. We had a lot of heart. We had a lot of strong characters too,' John adds.

'I always rib my mates who are Newcastle supporters about Mark McGhee and Micky Quinn. I tell them, "There's Mark McGhee and there's Micky Quinn." At this point John puts one of his hands into his right pocket and one of his hands into his left pocket. 'They didn't do anything because Benno and I didn't give them a chance,' John says. 'We did our jobs, and Eric and Marco did their jobs by scoring the goals. We all worked hard to get that 2-0 win. It was a very satisfying result because nobody expected us to do that. It ranks quite high on my all-time list of memories, particularly because we all got invited back to the George Washington hotel afterwards and Bob Murray said, "The champagne is on me!" That was a one-off!'

The prize for knocking out the Magpies was a play-off final against Swindon at Wembley, and a holiday for the first-team squad in Majorca.

'We went to Magaluf 10 days before the match and, looking back, I think the guys had too much to drink at that time, if I am honest,' John admits. 'It was supposed to be a time for relaxation, but perhaps some of the guys got a little bit over-zealous and started drinking too much. I think that maybe had something to do with it, because come the match against Swindon we really didn't perform very well.'

The day out at Wembley on a baking hot Spring Bank Holiday Monday was a glorious occasion for the Sunderland fans – up until 3 p.m.! The match was a one-sided affair, which Swindon completely dominated and easily won.

'There were 80,000 there that day and I would say it was easily three-to-one, maybe even four-to-one in favour of Sunderland supporters,' John says. 'I played at Wembley three times and I was never on the winning side. I got to the Freight Rover Trophy final with Bristol City, and we lost on penalties. I played in the Mercantile Credit Football Festival celebration for Sunderland against Wigan Athletic, and we lost on penalties. I scored from the spot in both of those matches. And then we had the match against Swindon, which was by far the biggest of the lot.

'The tunnel at Wembley could be deceptive,' John explains. 'You didn't hear anything from down below, even though there was 80,000 people singing their hearts out, you couldn't hear a thing down there. But when you walked up to the top of the tunnel and you saw daylight, that is when you heard this incredible roar.

'As for the match [Sunderland lost 1-0], we just weren't on the ball. It was very disappointing. I am just glad that Tony Norman was teetotal on the trip to Magaluf, otherwise it would have been 10-0. He had a great game at Wembley – thanks to us! I admit that Swindon were a good side, but we made them look like a good side as well. I hold my hands up to that.'

It felt as though it was an opportunity spurned for Sunderland, particularly after their fantastic achievement in winning the play-off semi-final against Newcastle. But, within days, rumours abounded about a possible demotion for Swindon due to illegal payments. As football fans up and down the country began to savour England's performances at Italia '90 and the antics of Gazza and Co., the Football League announced that Swindon would be relegated two divisions as a result of their inquiry and Sunderland would be promoted to the First Division in their place.

The game of football was torn. Some found it just, some found it unjust. Some argued Swindon should be fined, but retain First Division status; some argued Newcastle should replace them due to finishing third in the Second Division. Others argued that Sheffield Wednesday should retain First Division status and only two sides should be relegated in the circumstances. Sunderland remained silent and started to plan for a return to the top flight after a period of five years which had seen them fall all the way down to the Third Division and come all the way back.

'It had to be us,' John says. 'The Football League had to have faith in the play-off system. It didn't matter who finished third, fourth, fifth or sixth. It wasn't about that. They did it right, it was the right call.

'We all received bonus money for promotion,' John recalls. 'I splashed out on a family holiday to Fuerteventura. It cost me about £3,500 and we had a cracking time. I came back home, and when we got to the airport, I saw these big headlines saying "Swindon Joy". I couldn't believe it. I dropped my bags and picked up a paper. I feared the worst. I was also worried that I might have to give my bonus back, because I had spent over half of it!'

MacPhail did not need to worry. Although Swindon's demotion had been reduced on appeal, Sunderland were still going up. The Robins were relegated one division and, in effect, would therefore remain in the Second Division. Sunderland's promotion was confirmed. 'Phew!' John says with a smile, looking back.

During the summer of 1990 Denis Smith signed a new centre-half when he paid Portsmouth £350,000 for Kevin Ball.

It looked as though after three years, MacPhail's days as a Sunderland player were numbered.

Ball played in most of the pre-season matches, partnering Gary Bennett at the back, although he was not at his best, particularly against Torpedo Moscow at Roker Park. As a result the Sunderland manager made a late call and decided to give MacPhail his first match in the top flight of English football at the age of 34, away at Norwich City on the opening day of the season.

'I probably shouldn't have started,' John says. 'Denis Smith didn't play me in any of the pre-season games. Kevin Ball played in them all, but Denis wasn't very impressed with him. I think I came on as sub a couple of times, but no more. When he told me that he was going to play me against Norwich, I told him I was short of match practice. I scored an own goal, which didn't help, and I didn't feel as though I was at the races in that match. We lost 3-2, and it turned out to be my last game for Sunderland.

'On the Tuesday night we played Tottenham at home and drew 0-0. Kevin came back into the side and he played very well against the likes of Paul Gascoigne and Gary Lineker. Kevin kept his place from then on,' John says. 'Kevin is a good guy and a hard man. You don't mess with him. That is what you need, and you don't get that now. Having said that, if Kevin and myself were playing now, we would probably last about 10 to 15 minutes, because you can't tackle any more. Back then you could. But football has changed so much.'

MacPhail signed for Hartlepool United on 1 August 1990 and spent four years at Victoria Park, winning promotion in his first season as a player and culminating in a 10-month spell as manager.

'Cyril Knowles signed me for Hartlepool,' John remembers. 'He was a lovely man, but a hard man as well. He was worse than Denis Smith! They may have sung "Nice One, Cyril" about him, but it didn't necessarily go with him.

'When I got there, I was shocked. At Sunderland all your kit was always ironed and washed; at Hartlepool you had to take it home for your wife to wash it! After training, the players would run off to get to the bath first. It was: "Welcome to the real world." Now, I like the real world; I lived in a street in a place called Fintry in Dundee, which was not very pleasant, but as a Football League side Hartlepool were something else.

'I got the opportunity to manage them and I tried to take what I had learned from the likes of Harry Haslam, Terry Cooper and Denis Smith with me,' John adds. 'But it was a no-win situation. I had a £170,000 budget for 17 professional players, which worked out at £10,000 each. It was not enough. Money was a big problem there. I lasted less than a year in the job. Sadly, I felt that I was never given a chance to do it properly. It was an unhappy experience for me and it brought a cloud over my career after 24 years in the game. But last season, the Hartlepool chairman invited me to a match as his guest and I was given a standing ovation, which meant a lot to me. I spent five years there and I was voted their best centre-half, which was a nice accolade.

'A pal of mine at Sheffield United once told me, "When you get on the magic roundabout of managers, if you fall off it, it's very hard to get back on again." He was absolutely right,' John says.

In his career MacPhail played alongside many defenders who have links to Sunderland – Gary Bennett, David Moyes, Ricky Sbragia. So who does he consider was the best? 'I would probably say Gary Bennett,' John replies. 'He was an elegant player, cool and calm, and he scored some goals too. I played on the left and he played on the right – that was because he can't use his left foot! I just wish he would have stopped going on those mazy runs all the time, and leaving me to pick up three centre-forwards!'

6

Shaun Elliott was an outstanding defender for Sunderland from the mid-seventies to the mid-eighties. Capped by England at 'B' level he joined the ranks of Sunderland players who somehow did not win a full cap.

Elliott played over 350 times for the club, cruelly missed out on captaining Sunderland in the 1985 League Cup final through suspension and then moved to their cup-final conquerors Norwich.

Like numerous other players in this book Elliott's departure from Sunderland was not one he wanted. In his case he was simply shown the door by Lawrie McMenemy. Here, the man who was quicker than any Sunderland defender in living memory, talks about his time at Roker Park, his brilliant partnership with Jeff Clarke, and we discover how being one of 'Charlie's Angels' proved to be even more important after his boots were hung up . . .

SHAUN ELLIOTT

MEETS ROB MASON

Shaun Elliott was a tremendous defender whose 368 games between 1977 and 1985 place him 14th in the club's appearances list. Like so many homegrown youngsters – including Gordon Armstrong, who features later in *Tales of the Red and Whites* – Elliott emerged at what was a tough time for the club. He came into the side alongside fellow youngster Kevin 'Ossie' Arnott, and the pair joined Gary Rowell, another fledgling first-teamer. The trio were all discoveries of fabled scout Charlie Ferguson. As Elliott, Arnott and Rowell transformed a struggling side into an exciting one inevitably the youngsters were dubbed 'Charlie's Angels' after the hit TV show of the era.

Haltwhistle-born Elliott could, however, easily have been a Newcastle player. 'I went to play for Newcastle first of all,' he reveals, from his home near Norwich. 'I played one game up front for their juniors along with one of the other guys from our local team. I remember Alan Foggon played. I later met him but he wouldn't remember a game like that at Ponteland. He was a first-team player so I guess he'd been involved to gain a bit of fitness. We won about 5-0 and I scored two goals and hit the bar, so I did all right. I was still at school so I'd have been about 15 or 16.

'I never heard anything so I guess they thought I wasn't good enough, but I never got an option. I ended up going to Sunderland and playing for the team that was below their youth team. I'd have been about 16. Sunderland were great. They said,

"We're not going to judge you on one game. We're going to judge you over a few monthly periods." When Newcastle found out I was joining Sunderland they wanted to sign me but I'd made my mind up and I was always going to go to Sunderland. They always had a better reputation for kids when I was young so I stuck by them.'

Becoming an apprentice on his 17th birthday in January 1974 Shaun turned professional a year later but wasn't over-enamoured with every aspect of living the dream of a young player: 'My youth coach was a guy called Ray Yeoman. He was a bastard,' Elliott candidly admits. 'He was nasty to us all. There was only one guy that he really liked and that was Tony Maggiore. Ray Yeoman was bloody hard work.'

Hard work was evidently what the youth team of the time put in because there was a succession of young players being produced at that time. Gary Rowell and Mick Henderson had made their debuts in the season before Elliott's bow, while the 'Easington Express' Alan Brown, Tim Gilbert and Mick Coady also got their first opportunities in the same season as Shaun.

Elliott's big moment came a fortnight before his 20th birthday. Rooted to the foot of the First Division, Sunderland were seven games into a rotten record of 10 league games without scoring. They had managed to score twice the previous Saturday in an FA Cup tie where they'd been held 2-2 at home by Third Division Wrexham, renowned cup fighters of the period.

Jimmy Adamson, the former Burnley manager, had taken over the hot seat from Bob Stokoe in late 1976. Like so many managers before and since, at Sunderland and elsewhere, the new man wanted the old guard out and the his own men in. The home draw with Wrexham marked the last games of midfielder Ray Train and 1973 FA Cup hero Billy Hughes. Since Adamson's first match the previous month, Cup-winning full-back Dick Malone had also played his last match, while legendary keeper

Jim Montgomery was soon to be released. Others to have already come to the end of their Roker careers under Adamson included Alan Foggon, who had played alongside Elliott in that goal-scoring trial appearance Shaun had made in black and white.

Adamson's new-look Sunderland was to consist of a mixture of Burnley old boys and willing youngsters. As Elliott made his first appearance at Wrexham's Racecourse Ground he was soon joined by fellow debutant Kevin Arnott, who came off the bench. While the replay was lost 1-0 the youngsters impressed. Both started the next league game, a 2-0 loss at Leicester City. It was a ninth league defeat in a row, a penalty in the first game of that run being the only time Sunderland had scored. Adamson had been in charge for seven league games and was yet to see his side score a top-flight goal. Improvement came before the goals, a couple of goalless draws preceding a rare Friday-night fixture at home to Bristol City where a long-awaited goal from Mel Holden brought two points – three for a win were yet to come in.

Holden's goal was like flicking a switch. 'We had a little bit of a purple patch, with two sixes and a four,' says Shaun. Sunderland found that after all the weeks of nothing going in suddenly everything flew into the back of the net. Boro were blasted 4-0 before the Wests of Bromwich and Ham were each handed six of the best.

Elliott and Arnott had revitalised the side and, with both getting their first goals in that purple patch and Rowell rattling in a quarter of the 16 goals, Charlie's Angels had lift-off. 'It was one of those things where we were down and Jimmy Adamson brought the three of us in,' Elliott explains. 'We did well and we gave the whole area a little bit of hope. We were all local kids and we were all Sunderland fans – well, Ossie wasn't, he was a Newcastle fan, but never mind! Ossie was a couple of years younger than us. I did play with him at youth level but I would have been about 19 by then and he would have been about 17.'

Later in *Tales from the Red and Whites, Volume Two*, Gordon Armstrong talks about the development of young players and finding their best positions. Midfielder Armstrong debuted as a centre-back (when Elliott was injured), the only time he was asked to play there in over 400 Sunderland appearances. Equally, Elliott was a centre-back used in midfield in his early days, while so often people view Rowell as a striker, residing as he does in the esteemed company of Len Shackleton and Kevin Phillips as one of only three men with a century of post-war goals for the club. Rowell, though, is always ready to point out he played much of his career in his preferred role as a midfielder.

The verve and vivacity with which Charlie's Angels energised the Sunderland midfield was essential to the revival that saw the red and whites produce a 16-game run that included nine wins and two defeats. Had that run been from the start of the season, The Lads would have been challenging for the title. It was a far cry from the team that went ten games without a goal. From being cast adrift at the bottom of the 22-team division, Sunderland had scrambled to 16th with a game to go. West Ham, below them, won their last game, making the Hammers safe. So the final showdown came at Everton, where 36,000 congregated on a Thursday night – getting on for half of them from Sunderland, the crowd being 16,000 up on Everton's previous home gate. On the same evening Coventry City were entertaining Bristol City, where the attendance was also 36,000 – fewer than had seen the Sky Blues home game with Liverpool nine days earlier.

The scenario saw Sunderland's survival hopes resting on not losing at Everton but knowing that even if they did the losers of the Coventry v Bristol City game would be relegated. Only a draw in the game at Highfield Road combined with defeat for Sunderland could see Charlie's Angels brought to earth.

Sunderland had only failed to score once since their long barren run, which had ended over three months earlier but they could find no way past keeper Dai Davies, slipping to a disastrous 2-0 defeat. Meanwhile, at Coventry, the game had kicked off late, an arrangement allegedly constructed by Coventry's managing director Jimmy Hill. News of the Sunderland result was relayed via the scoreboard at Coventry where, with over 10 minutes to go, both teams were safe if there were no additions to the 2-2 scoreline. Coincidentally, Bristol City manager Alan Dicks was not only a former Coventry player but had been Jimmy Hill's assistant manager when Hill had been Coventry manager.

'I'll never forget that evening,' Elliott emphasises. 'It was bizarre. Everton had a great team and, even now, not many teams go to Everton and win there. I can remember walking around the dressing room in a daze. I was looking at people and the kids were in tears. We'd had such a good run in the last few months that I think everyone felt we might just scrape it, but we did have the toughest match of the lot as the last game of the season.

'I always used to look at the fixtures to see what the last game of the season was and Everton away was a tough one. It was like a bomb had gone off in our dressing room. People were just sitting there with their heads in their hands, there was kit and boots all over the place.

'Oddly enough Tom Ritchie played in that game for Bristol City. When he came to us I got to know him really well. He lived in Hexham, which was near me. We spoke about it often and he said nobody bothered to tackle and they just passed the ball around. They might as well have blown the whistle there and then. Nobody was going to score.'

So it was that the first full season Shaun would play would be in the equivalent of the current day Championship. Sixth place in that campaign would have meant a shot at the play-offs were they to have existed. There was a nearer promotion miss a year later when fourth place saw Sunderland miss out by a point in the tightest of races where, by now under caretaker-manager Billy Elliott [no relation], they finished just two points behind champions Crystal Palace.

Elliott missed only the opening day of that campaign, which featured Rowell's legendary hat-trick at Newcastle on a day when black and whiter Arnott carved open the Magpie defence time after time. Charlie's Angels may well have been plying their trade in the Second Division but heavenly performances such as this one are what made them so revered – on Wearside at least!

'A lot of my mates are Newcastle fans so you can imagine how that result went down,' smiles Shaun. 'That was a difficult thing for me, living on the Newcastle side. They put enough pressure on me to move nearer Sunderland but I was born and bred as a village lad. The thing was, when the game was over, come what may, I'd get a bit of ribbing and then it all settled down and even the Newcastle fans were good to me.

'The nucleus of the team was local, Gary was a Sunderland fan and so was I, although I did go to watch Newcastle occasionally. I watched Carlisle as well. I just went to see football. Joe Bolton was a local guy as well. We had bad games, but one thing you would always get from us was effort, even if it wasn't going right. One thing about Sunderland fans is that they appreciate effort: "You were crap today, but you worked hard." Compare it with Newcastle, when all the French guys came over. They were all right when they had the sun on their backs, but when it's wet and cold it becomes a different ball game.'

Five months almost to the day before the 4-1 win at St James' Rowell had to make do with just two goals in an almost equally

famous away victory. It came back at manager Jimmy Adamson's
old club, Burnley, where Adamson was fuming after seeing two
of his men sent off in a goalless first half only for nine-man
Sunderland to go out and win. 'Mickey Henderson had gone
first. David Merrington, the assistant manager, had gone in with
him and then Joe Bolton walked in and they asked, "Where's
the rest of the boys?" and Joe had to tell them, "I've been sent
off as well."'

Rowell rightly gets the glory as the goalscorer but obviously
playing with nine men meant that the unheralded defenders had
to be at their best, and by now Elliott was illustrating what a
fine defender he was. Always renowned for his pace and his
ability on the ball, bringing it out of defence as well as Alan
Hansen could at Liverpool, it can be forgotten what a tough
customer Northumbrian Elliott could be – and he had to be on
this occasion at Turf Moor. 'Big Stevie [Kindon] was playing up
front and was a bloody handful. He was huge that guy. A lovely
guy, and Leighton James was playing as well that day. Nobody
could believe it. It turned out to be a great result for the boss
and Dave Merrington [also ex-Burnley] and we did it with just
nine men.'

Partnering Elliott at the heart of Sunderland's defence in the
late seventies was Jeff Clarke. Elliott is not the best defender
Sunderland have had in my half century plus of watching the
team, and neither is Clarke, but both were top-class players
and, as a partnership, I rate them as the best central defensive
duo I've seen at the club: the Quinn and Phillips of defenders.
Clarke would be Quinny, big and commanding; Elliott would
be Phillips, the livewire who could handle himself and be first
to the ball when it mattered most – SuperShaun, if you like.
Elliott was Player of the Year in 1979 and Clarke a year later,
just as Quinn and Phillips won in successive seasons in the late

nineties, and the G-Force of Gates and Gabbiadini did so in consecutive years in the late eighties.

The Clarke-Elliott axis had its finest moments in the 1980 promotion season, although Elliott was often utilised in midfield with big Rob Hindmarch earning his place at the back. Sadly Clarke missed out on the denouement after a bad injury in the penultimate game at Cardiff City. Elliott's estimation of Clarke holds no bounds: 'The partnership with Jeff was the best I ever had. Jeff was a really good friend of mine as well. He was playing alongside Jackie Ashurst and I broke them up a little bit when I came in, which made me feel a bit sorry for Jackie. Jeff was built like a brick outhouse and before his injury he was fantastic. I played with a lot of guys – Russell Osman, Terry Butcher, and all them – but I honestly think if Jeff Clarke had never got injured he would have been an England international.

'Jeff had everything, and he had two bad injuries like the one that finished Brian Clough. I had pace and was fairly quick. We knew each other's games. I essentially knew if Jeff was going for it. I'd always cover him but I was asking myself, "Why am I covering him because he's just going to win that ball?" I think Jeff liked the idea of having me behind him so if anything did go wrong I was there. We had a great partnership. We were telepathic at times. We were just great friends. We roomed together, we socialised together. Jeff was just a great guy, and still is.

'People say was our partnership the best? I remember watching Dave Watson and Colin Todd. Toddy was one of my heroes. I never played for England but Toddy played a lot of times for England, so that tells a story. I wasn't as good as Colin Todd.'

Elliott's modesty is indicative of his character. He didn't lack confidence but he didn't big himself up either. He is as straightforward as his style of play was effective. Generally football gets faster with each generation, but I've still to see a forward faster over a short-sprint than Trevor Francis, who scored the winning goal in the European Cup final for Clough's Forest in the year before Sunderland's 1980 promotion, and I've yet to see a defender quicker at plugging the gaps than Elliott.

Had they played together more Dave Watson and Colin Todd may well have usurped Elliott and Clarke as Sunderland's best defensive duo, but between Watson's arrival as Sunderland's first £100,000 player just before Christmas 1970 and Todd becoming Britain's costliest defender when Clough captured him for Derby County less than two months later they only played in the same team four times – with Watson at centre-forward. Todd and Watson would go on to play together 18 times for England, however, with Dave in defence.

Watson started as a centre-half as a young lad, became a good centre-forward and eventually a great centre-half. Elliott began as a centre-forward as a youngster and was a good midfielder before becoming a great centre-back. He entertains no debate about his best position: 'Even though I came as a centre-forward I was always a centre-back. I always used to watch people in my position. When I was young I played up front, but they were local leagues so you didn't have to be special, if you know what I mean.'

Elliott had many attributes but feels he could have been better: 'I wish I was better on the ball. I remember watching Ajax play. Ruud Krol used to be my idol. He had everything and played with Cruyff. Krol was essentially a middle of midfield player playing at the back. That was unheard of then. When I was a kid you didn't get Sky or many televised games. You'd just see big European finals and internationals. At the time Ajax were the equivalent of a modern-day Barcelona.'

As Sunderland won the FA Cup just over six months before Shaun became an apprentice, Ajax were winning the European Cup for the third successive season. 'You could have put them all in a pot, picked them up and told any of them to play anywhere and they all would have been equally at home,' says Shaun, with undimmed admiration. 'They called it "Total Football", and it was.'

Back home, football remained a simple affair until the late seventies when Bobby Robson introduced the Dutch duo Arnold Mühren and Frans Thijssen at Ipswich around the time that Keith Burkinshaw brought Ossie Ardiles and Ricky Villa to Tottenham. Ken Knighton got as far as bringing Argentinian midfield maestro and future World Cup manager Alex Sabella to look around Sunderland but actually signed Claudio Marangoni, who failed completely to fit into a style of play that remained steadfastly English despite his introduction. He was good enough to win three major titles with Independiente and two international competitions with Boca Juniors after he was deemed not good enough for Second Division Sunderland!

'We always had people fairly quick up front, and all the coaches did was say, "Kick the ball over the full-backs." We never played like teams do now, through midfield,' says Shaun, who found a different approach when he played for Ken Brown at Norwich City half a decade later. 'When I went to Norwich I remember Brownie said, "See that guy there? Give him the ball. Don't kick it over the top." We had Dale Gordon and Ruel Fox up front, who were the quickest guys I'd ever seen, but Brownie had been a West Ham graduate and he wanted to play through midfield. Norwich still do now. They like to play football. It's all ifs and buts. If someone had spent a bit of time on me, developing my game as a young player, I might have played for England. Who knows?'

Surprisingly Shaun reveals that his game didn't develop in such a manner at Roker despite being under the tutelage of someone regarded as one of the country's finest coaches. Jimmy Adamson had coached England at the 1962 World Cup and had turned down the England manager's job before it was handed to Alf Ramsey. Adamson's young charges at Burnley were admired throughout the game for their style of play, but Shaun says, 'He was a lovely bloke, he really was, but he didn't do much coaching. What he did do was he stuck by his players, a bit like Ferguson or Wenger. Wenger says he never sees anything but I bet when he's talking in the dressing room he's seen it. He wouldn't embarrass you in front of the press or TV or anything though.'

Jimmy Adamson left Sunderland in the autumn of 1978 when the club were eighth in the division to take over as Jock Stein's successor at top-flight Leeds. Adamson was to resign from his position at Elland Road shortly before Elliott, Arnott and Rowell played their parts in beating what was essentially still his team 4-1 in the fourth home game after promotion in 1980, a result that took Sunderland to sixth in the table.

Shaun had missed just a single game as promotion was won under Ken Knighton in the season after Adamson vacated the Roker hot-seat but, like Roy Keane in a later era, for Elliott, success he took in his stride, while failure haunted him. 'When we got promotion it was great and I'll never forget it, but the ones that stick in my mind are the bad ones, like the Everton game,' he laments, even now.

Six weeks before promotion was secured with a 2-0 win over West Ham, who had won the FA Cup 48 hours earlier, Elliott had been a teammate of promotion-night opponent Alan Devonshire as his form was rewarded with international recognition. Playing alongside the likes of Bryan Robson, Viv Anderson and Paul Mariner, Shaun played for England at 'B' level against Spain: 'First of all when I was in the squad I thought, "Great!" But then I thought, "Was I picked because it's at Roker Park?" So that entered my mind. I felt a little bit out of my depth. Coming from the middle of Northumberland I was suddenly playing with all these guys who were household names.'

A decade later Marco Gabbiadini did indeed win his solitary England 'B' cap in a game at Roker (although Marco also twice played at Under-21 level) but Elliott impressed sufficiently in a 1-0 win to be selected the following season. He played in another 1-0 victory over the USA at Old Trafford, and in the return with Spain which was lost 3-2 in Granada. 'I was playing well and I felt as if I'd had a really cracking game that particular night at Roker, so then it gave me more confidence when I was chosen again. Later on Terry Venables and Bobby Robson tried to buy me – to go to Ipswich then. Apparently they'd been watching me for a while and said they would have loved to have had me in their teams. That gave me a huge boost to my confidence.'

That summer Shaun was indeed on the move – but only to the USA for a stint with Seattle Sounders with teammate Stan Cummins, who had sampled Stateside soccer before with Minnesota. 'I loved every minute of my time in Seattle,' says Shaun. 'I think we were out of contract, hence that's why we went. I was wanting a better contract than the club were prepared to offer me, which was unusual for me because I don't fight with anybody. When I'm off the pitch you've got to really do something bad to cheese me off, I'm the total opposite to being on the pitch. I've a friend down here in Norwich in Robert Fleck who is the same. He was a real bad-ass on the pitch but off the pitch you would not want to meet a nicer guy. He'd do anything for anybody. I loved it in Seattle. We enjoyed playing out there, made some nice money, saw the world and, for a single young kid out there, it was wonderful.'

It certainly was a refreshing change from a relegation battle with Sunderland. Given the scars from Everton four years earlier, Sunderland ended the first season after promotion

requiring victory on the other side of Stanley Park against a
Liverpool side due to face Real Madrid in the European Cup
final later that month. A goal from Cummins provided the
victory against Hetton lad Bob Paisley's Reds on an occasion
rumoured to be the one time Paisley was less than desperate
to see Liverpool win. 'We did play well that day,' recalls Shaun.
'Liverpool didn't want to let us beat them, but I don't think they
wanted to win either. It certainly wasn't high on their priorities.
When Stan scored the goal they didn't half put us under
pressure for an equaliser, but it was nice when we got some
chilled champagne afterwards.' There would be champagne for
Liverpool in Paris too – after Sunderland-born Alan Kennedy
scored their winner versus Real.

Making their final Sunderland appearances at Anfield
were Joe Bolton and – with Clarke still out – centre-half Sam
Allardyce. 'Big Sam was great to play with because he was so
commanding in the air, he was brilliant,' says Shaun. 'For a big
guy he had a nice touch as well. He was a bit like Jim Holton,
who I played with. They were like two peas in a pod. When Sam
left the England job I'd have broken the bank to get him back
as manager of Sunderland. He comes in when teams are shot,
near as dammit, and he always revives them. When he pulled
us around he did a fantastic job. That's why, if the England job
hadn't come around, he would have improved the team even
more.' Elliott is far from alone in that assessment.

Allardyce the manager is big on sports science – much of
which he learned during his own spells in America. There's no
way Big Sam the boss would let one of his key players spend
the summer playing in the USA after a long and demanding
season, but following his summer sojourn in Seattle Shaun had
to come back to Sunderland.

With fit again Jeff Clarke partnering Rob Hindmarch in
central defence Sunderland had begun well under new manager

Alan Durban, drawing away to Bobby Robson's UEFA Cup holders Ipswich Town and beating Aston Villa at home when Elliott got back, just as Sunderland were about to entertain West Ham. The night didn't go well for either the team, who lost, or Shaun, who got off to a less than auspicious start with the new boss: 'At the time when I'd left we didn't have a manager. I came back to Alan Durban being the new man in charge. All of the boys in our team in Seattle had a five-star hotel in Hawaii and I got told I had to come back, so I wasn't in a good frame of mind. I was getting a postcard every day of the next week from a different player sat on a beach somewhere in Maui! I walked back into the dressing room when I came back. It was the night of a game. I was jetlagged but I went to the match. Alan Durban saw me and said, "Hello, how are you? I'm Alan Durban and here's my midfield dynamo." That went down like a lead balloon, I must admit. I thought, "Oh, here we go" and our relationship was pretty much like that all the time he was there.'

Despite two and a half years of steady team building Durban was dismissed by chairman Tom Cowie to be replaced by former Sunderland defender Len Ashurst. What proved to be 'Lennie the Lion's' only full season in charge started so well but culminated in relegation and personal disappointment for Elliott.

Captain of the club, Shaun might have had dreams of emulating Bobby Kerr in raising aloft a trophy at Wembley only for fate to intervene. Sunderland were to lose the League Cup final to an own goal having missed a penalty, but Elliott was a spectator rather than a player, missing out on what should have been his big day through suspension.

Despite never having been sent off in his 368 games for Sunderland, an accumulation of yellow cards led to Elliott's Wembley woe, and Shaun vividly recalls the moment that cost him – and quite possibly cost Sunderland, as it was his teenage replacement David Corner's error that led to the only goal of the final. 'It came in the semi-final against Chelsea,' says Shaun. 'We'd beaten them 2-0 at our place in the first leg but at Stamford Bridge David Speedie broke through. I chased him. I was on his heels but not enough and I knew if I brought him down I was going to get booked. I just couldn't get in front or around the side of him. The box was coming up as we were running and, in a split second, everything went through my mind. I was thinking, "What's Chris [goalkeeper Chris Turner] doing?" and in the end, as the box came upon us I thought if I don't make an effort it'll be a penalty in a moment and, of course, I brought him down. Funnily enough if it had been by today's rules I'd have been off and I'd have been OK for the final because there were other games to play so the suspension would have been served. Everything was going through my mind because I was thinking, "I want to play at Wembley, I might not get there again." That night wasn't the best for me, although it was all right when I was drunk on champagne in Stringfellows!'

Being suspended for a final is greater torture for a player than missing out through injury, although even if Shaun hadn't been suspended he might have missed out anyway: 'I'd been involved in the build-up but I never felt part of it. We'd gone down a few days before and when we had our breakfast together I felt a bit out of it. Oddly enough I got a bit of a bug down there and I felt really rough. I couldn't travel home. There were a couple of us stayed down although I think in Peter Daniel's case he was probably hungover! I felt really awful the next day. It might have been psychological because all week I was thinking, "What the hell am I doing here? Because I can't play."'

A decade on from when they were teammates at youth level Elliott and Gary Rowell watched Norwich's lap of honour together along with injured Sunderland midfielder Mark Proctor. Rowell had moved on to Norwich the previous summer but had endured an injury-hit season and was on crutches. To this day Rowell is such a red and white supporter it doesn't bear thinking that he might have played and scored. 'We shared some good times but unfortunately we did share a few bad times, Gary and myself,' reflects Shaun of the dying embers of an era when Sunderland had been built on homegrown talent.

By the end of one more season Shaun would also be treading the path to Carrow Road. Both Sunderland and Norwich were relegated in the season they met in the League Cup final, Ashurst being replaced at Roker by Lawrie McMenemy.

'We got guys like Frank Gray, Alan Kennedy and Eric Gates, who were seasoned internationals,' says Shaun of Lawrie Mac's policy of bringing in big-name veterans. 'At the time, I'd been there for about 12 years and I was due a testimonial. We ended up nearly going down for two years running and I was thinking, "I can't have a testimonial, no one will turn up."

'Chris [Turner] and I had been good performers over many years. Well, you can't tell me these guys were on less wages than us, so me and Chris were hacked off to a certain extent. We were thinking, "Hang on a minute, we were fighting over a few quid." The guys were great guys. We didn't have anything against them. In fact, we got on really well with them because they were all nice guys. It just rocked the club a little bit. Lawrie was on a king's ransom as well.'

Turner left for a club-record-equalling sale, joining Manchester United before most of McMenemy's men arrived. Elliott would have one more season at Sunderland – McMenemy's first. It was an utter disaster. Chairman Sir Tom Cowie had pulled off a coup in attracting McMenemy, who was one of the biggest names in the game, but when the team began with five defeats without scoring a goal, optimism vanished. Relegation to the Third Division was avoided only with the help of back-to-back-wins without conceding in the final two fixtures. They were to be the last games Shaun played for Sunderland, but he didn't see the move coming: 'It was bizarre. I just got told "Brownie [Norwich manager Ken Brown] wants to speak to you, you better go." Durban tried to sell me to Burnley when John Bond was manager as well. I didn't have a choice. It was all very abrupt. It just happened. When you see a transfer now it seems to be in the paper for a week before it goes through. I didn't want to leave Sunderland ever. If someone had come along I'd have probably said no. The only reason I left was because Lawrie told me to go.'

The players in this book are all chosen because they were good players for Sunderland. In numerous cases they are players whose stories haven't been explored as much as their place in club history warrants. A further thing that connects several of them, including Elliott, is this scenario where their departure from the club was something that made them as unhappy as the supporters who didn't want to see good players like Shaun Elliott, Darren Holloway, Martin Scott and Stan Anderson sold.

Having missed out on what would have been his biggest day as Sunderland skipper by being suspended for the 1985 League Cup final, Shaun's transfer, ironically, was to replace the captain who had lifted the trophy that day, Norwich's Dave Watson. The namesake of Sunderland's 1973 FA Cup-winning defender had moved from Norwich to Everton. 'I got some stick for that, trust me,' says Shaun. 'Obviously they had beaten us in the cup final, but prior to that, when I played, we won at Carrow Road the week before, so that was my comeback.'

Having played alongside a future Sunderland manager at Roker Park in Sam Allardyce, Elliott partnered another at Carrow Road in Steve Bruce: 'We were two northerners in the same place. We got on famously well and so did the girls. We never had long periods together like I did with Jeff because Steve got injured and then so did I.'

Relegated together after the League Cup final, while Sunderland had dropped like a stone, Norwich had bounced back into the top flight as champions. In Elliott's first season City impressively finished fifth, although after being a regular in the first part of the season injury limited him to just two league appearances after November.

The following season he managed just over a third of the games, often in the unfamiliar role of left-back, and at the end of the season was on the move once more, this time teaming up again with goalkeeper Barry Siddall at Third Division Blackpool: 'Baz was there. He was a big imposing character. He used to torture the people he didn't get on with, but he was great, and a great keeper,' laughs Shaun, who suffered relegation with the Tangerines in his second season. Elliott moved on to Colchester in 1991, signing for Ian Atkins only for his old Sunderland teammate to soon depart as the U's finished runners up in the Conference, going on to win it a year later with Shaun almost ever present.

By now in his mid-thirties the final days of Elliott's playing career were back in the north-east with Gateshead, Bishop Auckland, Whitley Bay and Durham City. Rather like Julio Arca turning out for the Willow Pond pub and subsequently becoming a Wembley winner with South Shields in 2017, Shaun was a player who just wanted to keep playing for as long as his legs would allow him. 'Absolutely,' he agrees, 'I would have played for Sunderland for nothing, so would people like Gary Rowell and Joe Bolton. That was the mentality I had. Money has never been my god. I just loved playing football and if you can pass a little bit on to young kids who are just starting then so be it. I've been to America coaching kids and it's given me great satisfaction to see kids make big improvements. I just enjoyed playing football. I was at Albany as player-coach with Paul Mariner. It's a town in New York State.'

In more recent years Shaun has worked in the motor trade in the Norwich area. Back in 2015, a week before his 58th birthday, he suffered a major health scare when a blood clot in an artery – he was already in an ambulance having complained of chest pains – led to emergency treatment: 'It wasn't a pleasant evening for me and it wasn't for my family either. There's no two ways about it. If the paramedic wasn't with me I wouldn't be here now. My heart stopped beating and he got it going again. I feel a little bit blessed because of that, I must admit. The surgeon when I went straight to surgery said, "I know who you are, Shaun. I suppose you're wondering what you're doing here?" I replied, "The thought had crossed my mind, I must admit. I've not put weight on, I've never been a big drinker, I've never been a smoker and I'm a fisherman so I eat fish not meat – so what am I doing here?"

'It was just one of those things. You look at Ugo Ehiogu and what happened to David Ginola [whose heart stopped for eight minutes before he was revived]. I was luckier than those guys. What had happened was that one of the main arteries to my heart was blocked. They had to resuscitate me and take the blockage out. It took me a long time to get over it. It took a year. My doctor said, "Shaun, you're not a 20-year-old footballer any more."'

That's true, but thankfully when one of Charlie's Angels needed angels of his own the East of England Ambulance Service came to the rescue.

7

Tony Towers won a European Cup-Winners' Cup medal with Manchester City a fortnight after his 18th birthday.

Four years later he was part of the £225,000 player-exchange deal that took two of Sunderland's 1973 FA Cup heroes – Dennis Tueart and Micky Horswill – to Maine Road. He led Sunderland to the Second Division championship in 1976, and went on to win three England caps at the end of that season. His departure for Birmingham City a year later was a massive disappointment to many Sunderland fans. Now, 40 years on, he reveals here that he never wanted to leave Roker Park.

TONY TOWERS

MEETS LANCE HARDY

The early summer of 1976 was a good time to be a Sunderland supporter: Second Division champions, back in the First Division after six long years, and international recognition for our star player and club captain, Tony Towers, who played three times for England in just 20 days.

Towers was my favourite player when I was a boy; I even had a *Shoot!* poster of him on my bedroom wall. He seemed to have everything in his game: the perfect pass, a strong tackle, time, skill, vision and scoring ability. Plus he was captain of the club I loved and he took all the penalties. I remember being thrilled when he played for England in the Home International Championship, particularly as it came less than a month after Sunderland's successful promotion campaign. It felt as though England manager Don Revie had personally recognised the club's return to the big time.

Of course, Dave Watson had represented England in the 1975 Home Internationals for England while he was still a Sunderland player. But he only remained so for a matter of days: soon he would be playing for Manchester City, joining the likes of Colin Todd and Dennis Tueart as former Red and Whites proudly wearing the Three Lions on their shirts but playing in the First Division for other clubs.

This felt different. It was like a new beginning. Maybe there was an element of naïvety on my part, but when the First Division fixtures for 1976-77 came out, it really did feel as though it was the beginning of a new chapter for Sunderland. The official team photograph, with Towers sitting in the middle of the front row with the Second Division trophy in between his knees, suggested a much brighter future after the frustration of the post-1973 FA Cup triumph hangover years. It was only later that we found out about Roy Greenwood being banned from appearing in the photograph because he refused to shave off his beard! In hindsight that rather puerile and ridiculous reaction by the highly popular and idolised Sunderland manager Bob Stokoe suggests that something wasn't quite right at Roker Park. And so it transpired. But, while it lasted – regardless of the furore in the letters page of the *Sunderland Echo* over Roy Greenwood's beard and his omission from the pre-season snaps – it was certainly a magical summer to be a Sunderland fan.

All these years on I am sitting in Prestwich, a suburb three miles north of Manchester city centre, with Tony Towers, reminiscing about that halcyon summer, when the sun never stopped shining, but that was a special Sunderland side too . . .

Towers was born and raised in Manchester. He could have signed for Matt Busby's Manchester United at the age of 13, but his father was a scout for Manchester City, and he advised him to join the blue revolution that had just got underway at Maine Road under Joe Mercer and Malcolm Allison. He signed schoolboy forms in 1965, when City were still in the Second Division. But the following season they were promoted as champions, and in 1967-68 they won the First Division title. The following year they beat Leicester City 1-0 at Wembley to win the FA Cup, and in 1970 they beat West Bromwich Albion 2-1 at Wembley to win the League Cup, as well as Górnik Zabrze of Poland, 2-1 in the rain in Vienna, to win the UEFA European Cup-Winners' Cup.

Towers was one of the most successful of Mercer and Allison's protégées. He made his debut in the First Division with

City just five days after his 17th birthday, and won a European Cup-Winners' Cup winners' medal with them just a fortnight after his 18th birthday. Four years on he also played in the 1974 League Cup final, which City lost 2-1 to Wolverhampton Wanderers. But, by then, Mercer and Allison were both gone and Ron Saunders was in charge. Within a fortnight Towers was signed by Bob Stokoe for Sunderland in the £225,000 plus player-exchange deal which also took Dennis Tueart and Micky Horswill to Maine Road. Just over two years later he led the Rokerites to the Second Division title under 'the Messiah'. Stokoe's Stars had finally reached the First Division . . .

'We had a very good team at Sunderland,' Tony says. 'There was a strong camaraderie, we all stuck together and every one of us gave 100 per cent. What helped so much was that the squad was such a good bunch of lads with plenty of characters. We were a good set of friends, actually.

'Whenever we trained at Roker Park a group of about six or seven of us always went to this Italian café on a corner nearby called Ricky's. We used to say, "Ricky, get us our usual" as soon as we walked in. Billy Hughes would have his mince and tatties, and Vic Halom and I would have mince and chips, with a cup of tea to go with it. It was a bit of a culture shock for me at first, but it was really good as well.

'The core of that team had been together for quite a long time when I joined in 1974. A lot of them had won the FA Cup in 1973, of course. We were always challenging to get promoted over the next few seasons, and in the end we finally got up. It was a good time and, of course, personally, 1976 was an excellent year for me.

'I remember my first England call up very well. We were playing Oldham Athletic, and it was quite a tough game with a lot of kicking and things like that,' Tony recalls. 'I didn't know it at the time but Don Revie, the England manager, and his assistant Les Cocker were in the stands watching me. Lo and behold a few days later a nice letter arrived at the club saying that I had been invited to go down to a training session with the full England squad. It came completely out of the blue.

'I was selected to play in an Under-23 match first of all, before the 1976 Home International Championship. Don Revie gave me a role to mark this player out of the game. Afterwards he came up to me, looked me in the eye and told me that I would be playing against Wales at Ninian Park. I was gobsmacked.'

The Sunderland captain was one of three new caps in Cardiff that day, along with Manchester United duo Brian Greenhoff and Stuart Pearson. In the England line-up only Ray Clemence and Kevin Keegan had more than 10 caps to their name. But that was often Revie's way at that time: in England's previous match, also against Wales just six weeks earlier, he had given first caps to no fewer than eight players.

The match was watched by a crowd of just 24,592 – less than half of some Sunderland crowds that season – and Peter Taylor, who was playing in the Third Division with Malcolm Allison's Crystal Palace, scored the only goal of the game for England.

'Looking back now, that game is largely a blur,' Tony admits. 'Don Revie wanted me to do the same job on Terry Yorath in the Wales midfield as I had done in the Under-23s match for him. I don't think I played too well, actually. I think I gave him too much space. If I had had a good game, I think I might have been set up going forward with England.'

Three days later Towers came on as a second-half substitute for England against Northern Ireland in a 4-0 win in front of a 48,000 crowd at Wembley. He didn't play in the final match of the Home International Championship against Scotland at Hampden Park, which England lost 2-1, but he was on the plane to America for the US Bicentennial Tournament, featuring Brazil, Italy and an invitational Team America, the following week.

'It was great to be involved in that,' Tony says. 'Brazil and Italy were two of the best teams in the world and the US side featured a lot of North American Soccer League players who were out there at that time.'

Towers didn't play in England's opening match of the series, a 1-0 defeat to Brazil in Los Angeles, but he started in the second match against Italy at Yankee Stadium in New York. At half-time England trailed 2-0 to two Francesco Graziani strikes, but they hit back to win 3-2 with two goals from Mick Channon and one from Phil Thompson, all scored within eight minutes of the restart.

'That was a really fantastic occasion,' Tony adds. 'To be 2-0 down to Italy and then winning 3-2, in such a great atmosphere too. I found New York to be a very cosmopolitan city, and the fans who were there that day understood their football and filled the stadium. I had a bit of a tussle with Giancarlo Antognoni during that match. He snapped a chain off my neck. I think we both got booked. He got substituted afterwards and then he had a go at his manager, Enzo Bearzot, as he walked off. I don't know what he said – it was in Italian!

'Our final match of that tour was in Washington against the all-American team, who had Pelé and Bobby Moore playing for them. I wasn't selected, but we won the game 3-1. So we finished second in the table, behind Brazil. I really enjoyed that whole tour with England. It was a fantastic experience and Don Revie was absolutely brilliant: he always went into so much detail on the opposition, and he knew everything about them.

'It was a good time,' Tony recalls. 'I thought I was going to keep on playing for England, and I was looking forward to playing in the First Division with Sunderland as well.'

After an exhilarating month with England, Towers' focus shifted back to Sunderland and the forthcoming First Division campaign. Bob Stokoe had publicly stated during the summer that he wanted to bring in four new signings to the club. Unfortunately when the season kicked off in August, away at Stoke City, he had been unable to add to his squad at all.

'I think it was probably the same as it is now: it was hard to get a lot of players to come to Sunderland,' Tony says. 'The club was always on the threshold of going up, staying up, going back down and so on.'

The first three games of the new season were all drawn, but then came a sequence of defeats that left Sunderland bottom of the table by the middle of September. The signs were that they were already in for a long relegation scrap.

'It just seemed to be that we kept getting beaten 1-0 a lot in the early part of that particular season, if I remember rightly, when we could have perhaps won or drawn some of those games,' Tony recalls. 'We didn't have too much luck going for us and, before we knew it, we were at the bottom of the table.'

Before they knew it, they were also without a manager. Stokoe surprisingly resigned in mid-October following a 1-0 home defeat to Aston Villa. Despite the best efforts of Sunderland chairman Keith Collings, the Messiah declined to change what was a difficult, heartfelt decision. In the meantime Sunderland remained at the bottom of the table, without a win to their name.

'I don't really know what happened there,' Tony says. 'I couldn't get my head around it at the time. Bob Stokoe was a very passionate person and he was quite an emotional man as well. If things didn't go right I know he would often get these migraines. But I don't know why he resigned all of a sudden like that. Maybe he just felt that he couldn't do any more?

'It was very sad because he was such a great character and a fantastic manager as well,' Tony adds. 'His assistant, Arthur

Cox, was a really nice guy too. He used to do all the warm-ups and everything with us, even though we very rarely went outside on the pitch, maybe because it was always freezing up there! So, most of the time, we were indoors, doing all our drills, fitness and five-a-sides. Bob would play with us and it would get competitive. Bob was always competitive!'

Towers was still only 21-years-old when Stokoe brought him up to Roker Park. It was something of a complicated, drawn-out transfer, but that glorious Manchester City era under Mercer and Allison, which burned so brightly in the late 1960s, was over and it was time to move on. The new man in charge at Maine Road, Ron Saunders, had his own ideas – although, as it turned out, not for much longer, for he was to be sacked three weeks before the end of the 1973-74 season.

'I had a very successful and exciting time at Manchester City, winning trophies and everything,' Tony says. 'Those were great days; Joe Mercer was the figurehead while Malcolm Allison did all the training with us. He was a flamboyant character and an excellent coach as well. He was very good with his players, and treated us all like men. He was absolutely fantastic with the youngsters as well, coming back in the afternoons to train them all himself. We never finished until about 4.30 p.m. when Malcolm was there. It was really good and we were very successful.

'But then Joe left and Malcolm did it on his on for a while,' Tony adds. 'I think Joe was a bit disappointed with the way it all happened, but the players didn't know too much about it, it was just one of those things. We obviously knew that Malcolm was a fantastic coach, but he didn't remain there too long on his own. Apparently, one reason why he left us was that he felt he couldn't get any more from his players, but he didn't want to sell them either. Players like Francis Lee, Mike Summerbee,

Neil Young or whoever, had done everything for him, and he didn't want to have to break that team up.'

Towers remembers the day when Stokoe called Manchester City to speak to him for the first time about a possible move to Sunderland very well.

'I got a call to go into the club, and I was told it was because Ron Saunders wanted to have a chat with me,' Tony explains. 'I soon found out why: Sunderland were interested in signing me.

'Apparently they had come in for me before. I knew all about them because of the 1973 FA Cup win, of course. We played against them twice in the fifth round that year and I remember their support was phenomenal.

'I remember scoring in the first match at Maine Road and then getting myself sent off after clashing with Micky Horswill – I was actually expecting Micky to join me and I was waiting for him in the tunnel, but he didn't get sent off,' Tony laughs. 'That is just how it was in those days – it was start at the neck and work your way down when you tackled; take a look at Bestie when Chopper Harris tried to scythe him down.

'Anyhow, Ron Saunders told me that Bob Stokoe wanted to talk to me. So, I went on the phone, I listened to what Bob had to say and I said to him, "Thanks very much, but no thanks." I felt settled at Manchester City; I had just got married, I had just bought a new house and my wife was expecting . . . so it was thanks, but no thanks.'

But that wasn't the end of this story, nor was it even half of this story. At the same time, back in the north-east, one of Sunderland's 1973 heroes, Dennis Tueart, had been transfer-listed at his own request after a disappointing start to the season by the FA Cup holders. Stokoe told Tueart that he would sell him on one condition: that he could organise a player-exchange.

As the late-season transfer deadline approached, the possibility of such a deal being agreed between Sunderland

and Manchester City increased, with firm interest coming from Maine Road in both Tueart and Micky Horswill. Tueart recalls being told to turn up at Roker Park one morning, and along with Horswill and Stokoe, he was driven to Wetherby by Sunderland chairman Keith Collings to meet Saunders, his assistant Tony Book, and City chairman Peter Swales to discuss terms. When the deal was done, Sunderland got Towers and £225,000, and City got Tueart and Horswill.

'I didn't know the other parts to it, but it was all down to me agreeing to go,' Tony says. 'Sunderland wanted me or the deal wasn't going to go ahead. It went on and on, and Sunderland kept upping the money and, in the end, I signed for them.

'Yes, it was a drop into the Second Division for me, but I felt as though Sunderland would soon get promoted,' Tony adds. 'The Sunderland supporters were a big factor as well. There was a tremendous following for Sunderland in those FA Cup games in 1973, and I had seen it with my own eyes.'

Unsurprisingly, Sunderland had been priced as massive favourites to win promotion after their incredible Wembley win, but the side lost momentum in the 1973-74 season. Furthermore, Stokoe was heavily criticised for fielding weakened teams during the league campaign as his squad competed in three major cup competitions, including the European Cup-Winners' Cup, which was to be the club's first and, as things stand, last sojourn into senior European competition. Ultimately, the plan to rest senior players in Second Division matches backfired and by the start of the new year Sunderland were placed in the bottom half of the table. They were also out of the FA Cup, League Cup and Europe.

On the day Towers signed, Sunderland were in 10th place in the Second Division with 10 league matches left. He immediately helped to contribute to an improved run of seven wins and a draw which pushed them up to a final position of sixth, just two points below a promotion spot in the end. He also scored his first goals for the club in the last two games, against Blackpool and Luton Town. But 14 league defeats – one-third of all matches played – told its own story that season.

'I have to admit it was a big culture shock for me when I got up there,' Tony laughs. 'Sunderland put me up at the Roker Hotel on the seafront at first, looking out towards the North Sea. Well, the wind was blowing and there were blinking gales and everything. My room was damp as well, and I did start to think to myself, "What have I done here?" I had gone from a First Division club, winning European Cup-Winners' Cup medals, League Cup medals and Charity Shield medals, to this!

'But in the end it brought the best out of me, because from the age of 13 when I had first joined Manchester City, everything had been done for me, right through to England schoolboys and playing for one of the top clubs in the country,' Tony adds. 'Coming up to Sunderland made me grow up, and once I had found my feet, it was great for me. Bob Stokoe and the directors would do anything for you, that's important to mention too. We moved into our house in South Hylton, down on the river, and the people there were absolutely fantastic. We became settled there. My little lad was born up in Sunderland, and the missus loved it.'

Sunderland still had the nucleus of their 1973 FA Cup-winning side, and the popular signings of Towers and, in the summer of 1974, former Newcastle United and West Ham United striker Pop Robson, strengthened the squad significantly following the departure of Tueart and Horswill.

'Big Dave Watson was still there; Billy Hughes, Vic Halom, Bobby Kerr were still there; plus Jim Montgomery, Dick Malone and so on,' Tony recalls. 'We had a very good attacking side and that's the way Bob Stokoe always wanted us to play. We loved to get forward, make chances and score goals.'

Sunderland were priced as second-favourites to win promotion ahead of the 1974-75 season, just behind Tommy Docherty's relegated Manchester United, a team that featured a number of talented young players alongside the likes of Alex Stepney, Martin Buchan, Lou Macari, Willie Morgan and Stuart Pearson.

Famously, the two sides met at Old Trafford on a cold November day in 1974, positioned first and second in the table, in front of a massive attendance of 60,585. It was to be a classic encounter, played in front of a fervent crowd: Sunderland trailed 1-0, led 2-1 and eventually lost 3-2. The game was shown on *Match of the Day* and at the end of the season it was voted Match of the Season by BBC viewers. Furthermore, Docherty proclaimed that his fellow countryman, Billy Hughes, who scored both of Sunderland's goals that day, was 'the most exciting player in Britain' after his stunning performance.

The quality on show was something else: Sunderland's line-up was their 1973 FA Cup final team with only Towers, Robson and Bobby Moncur in place of Horswill, Tueart and Ritchie Pitt, while six of the Manchester United side would be in the team that beat Liverpool to win the FA Cup in 1977.

'That was a really fantastic game,' Tony recalls.' It was a full house. United always have a full house, of course, but Sunderland could take something like 12,000 to 15,000 supporters away with them in the Second Division at that time, and that day was no different.'

'How did you win the Cup?' goaded the Manchester United fans after Pearson had given them an 11th-minute lead. 'That's how we won the Cup,' replied the Roker Roar (on tour in Manchester) two minutes later after Hughes and Robson had combined breathtakingly and beautifully to make it 2-1. On the following Monday, the *Daily Mirror* asked in an exhaustive match report: 'Who will go up with the pair of them?'

The answer would be that only one of them would go up. Sunderland missed out on promotion once again, this time finishing fourth, two points behind the top-three places once again. Two defeats in the last three games sealed the club's fate.

However, there was also another reason . . . Seven days after the match at Old Trafford, following a 4-1 win over Portsmouth at Roker Park, Ian Porterfield, the 1973 FA Cup final goalscoring hero, had been seriously injured in a car crash on the outskirts of Sunderland. He suffered a fractured skull in the accident and didn't play again for the rest of the season. Towers believes this had a huge impact on the team.

'Ian's car crash affected us quite badly,' Tony says. 'It was a very serious accident and it was touch and go for a while whether he would make it. Thankfully, he did, but he never returned to the player he was.'

At the end of the 1974-75 season Dave Watson signed for Manchester City for £275,000. It was a blow, but part of the deal saw the impressive Jeff Clarke come to Sunderland in another player-exchange. Clarke became an ever-present in the side until he sustained a bad injury at Orient in March which curtailed his season. Another new signing, Mel Holden, picked up for £100,000 from Preston North End, was an instant hit in front of goal.

'We had a very good team by that time,' Tony recalls. 'We had good balance in the side, there was plenty of skill, plenty of goals, and we worked our socks off for each other.'

Sunderland, with Towers, Holden and Robson all reaching double figures in the goal charts, were well on course for promotion this time round. For a while it looked as though they might have even been on course for a unique Second Division title and FA Cup double as well.

After beating two other Second Division sides, Oldham Athletic and Hull City, in the third and fourth rounds,

Sunderland went to First Division Stoke City and drew 0-0 in front of a crowd of 41,176 at the Victoria Ground, bolstered by another huge following from the travelling supporters. Towers cleared a Jimmy Greenhoff shot off the line.

Four days later Sunderland, with goals from Holden and Robson, knocked Stoke out, winning 2-1 in front of 47,583 spectators. Three years on from shocking the nation, FA Cup fever was well and truly back on Wearside, particularly as the quarter-final draw brought Third Division Crystal Palace to Roker Park, and the old stadium now had an unbeaten home record in major competitions stretching all the way back to April 1974.

But former Everton striker Alan Whittle was to ruin the party, scoring the only goal of the game for Palace in the second half. Dennis Longhorn hit the bar for Sunderland. The crowd was 50,850. Most of them walked away from the ground at the end of the match in disbelief and disappointment. The Third Division side, under Towers' old manager, the flamboyant Malcolm Allison, were now causing an FA Cup sensation of their own after wins at Leeds United, Chelsea and Sunderland.

'That was a big lost opportunity for us, there is no doubt about it,' Tony recalls. 'We reached the quarter-finals of the FA Cup and we were at home to a Third Division side with a place in the semi-finals at stake. It was a dream of a draw for us but, unfortunately, we lost.

'Malcolm Allison was there with his big hat on and his cigar, playing it up in front of the crowd,' Tony adds. 'It was a really big shock for us to lose that game and a really big disappointment as well. I think we played better than Palace on the day, but they got the all-important goal. We had a good chance of doing that Double; we were confident that we were going to win the Second Division and we thought we could get to the FA Cup final as well.'

To rub salt into Sunderland's wounds, Palace were then drawn against Southampton, another Second Division side, in the semi-final, avoiding the two fancied First Division clubs, Manchester United and Derby County. Southampton beat Palace 2-0 at Stamford Bridge and then went on to beat United 1-0 in the final.

'Southampton finished well below us in the table that season,' Towers says. 'But they went on to win the FA Cup.'

Sunderland had achieved promotion the previous month with a 2-1 home win over fourth-placed Bolton Wanderers. The match was watched by another huge crowd of 51,983 fans. Ground capacity was gradually reduced over the next 20 years or so, and it remains the last time Sunderland played a home match with an attendance above 50,000.

Stokoe's Stars had finally done it! Towers and Robson scored the goals that day. It had taken Sunderland six long years to return to the top flight following relegation under Alan Brown in 1970. Their home league form had been magnificent all season: 19 wins and just two draws – against both Bristol clubs – in 21 matches.

'That tells you why we were so disappointed to lose to a Third Division side at home in the FA Cup quarter-finals!' Tony shrugs with a smile.

Towers contributed 10 goals during that league campaign. Five of them came from the penalty spot, including one in the promotion-clinching match against Bolton.

'It was a responsibility that I took on at Sunderland,' Tony says. 'Francis Lee always took the penalties at City, but I was always pretty confident taking them.'

In total, Towers scored 11 times from the spot for the Red and Whites. Another of those penalties came early in the following season in a marathon League Cup encounter against Manchester United, watched by a total of almost 125,000 spectators over three matches. Sunderland finally succumbed after a second replay.

'I remember those night games against United very well,' Tony recalls. 'I vividly remember the first match at Old Trafford. I scored in that one and I scored in the first replay as well. They were two exciting 2-2 draws, but we lost out when we played them for a third time.'

Ten days after that League Cup defeat came Stokoe's surprise resignation. By that time Sunderland were well and truly in a relegation battle, with just four points from their opening nine games.

Just before he left, Stokoe did add to his squad, signing goalkeeper Barry Siddall and striker Bob Lee, and also bringing in Scottish international centre-half Jim Holton on loan. But it all happened too late to persuade him to stay in the job.

'We didn't have a great start that season and that never helps,' Tony recalls. 'I was struggling badly with a thigh injury early on as well, and it went on for a long, long time. Gary Rowell came into the side in my place and he was fantastic. Later on Kevin Arnott and Shaun Elliott came into the team as well, and the results began to pick up for us. We had a very young side, and that was all down to the new manager.'

Jimmy Adamson was appointed Sunderland manager in early December 1976 after a seven-game caretaker stint by Stokoe's assistant, Ian MacFarlane. Jim Montgomery and Bobby Moncur had by now played their last games for the club. Adamson oozed confidence on his arrival, but he was to witness a club record run of 10 league games without scoring a goal, which included eight straight defeats and two goalless draws, that lasted until mid-February.

Sunderland also crashed out of the FA Cup to Third Division Wrexham in a third-round replay in January 1977. Towers missed both games against the Welsh side through his troublesome injury, which limited him to only five appearances between the end of December and the beginning of April.

'It wasn't an easy time for me,' Tony admits. 'At one stage, the club told me to go away and have a rest, so I went up to the Lakes for a bit with the wife and kiddies. My injury gradually got better, but it was a frustrating time.'

By the time he returned, Adamson had decided to throw in the youngsters and, astonishingly, it almost saved Sunderland during the second half of what was to become the ultimate rollercoaster of a season. Once they had finally found the net (after two-and-a-half long months without a league goal) they couldn't stop: Middlesbrough were beaten 4-0, West Bromwich Albion were defeated 6-1, and West Ham were thrashed 6-0 within a fortnight. It was an incredible turnaround.

Towers missed each of those games due to his recurrent thigh injury, but when he returned to the Sunderland side in early April at Leeds United, the team were now on an unbeaten run of nine matches, which pushed them out of the relegation zone. Towers played in a defensive role at Elland Road, in place of Colin Waldron. He returned to the midfield in the following match, a 2-1 win over Manchester United at Roker Park, where he scored yet another penalty. In total, he played in the final seven of those nine unbeaten games, scoring four goals in three wins and four draws.

As is well-known (I wrote about it in *Tales from the Red and Whites, Volume One*), Sunderland went to Everton in their final game of that delirious and exhausting season, two places above the bottom three and needing just a draw to avoid relegation. Furthermore, they would have survived even if they had lost, providing there was a winner in the other match that night between the two other relegation-threatened sides, Coventry City and Bristol City, who were to play each other at Highfield Road.

Sunderland lost 2-0 and Coventry and Bristol City drew 2-2, after a controversially delayed kick-off, to relegate the Rokerites. It is a story that will be passed down for generations to come. There were tears on the terraces and much worse at and around Goodison Park that night as the sad, frustrating reality of what had actually happened slowly reverberated around the visiting supporters. There were tears in the Sunderland dressing room too, but it is possible that the most frustrated player in there might well have been the club captain, who was surprisingly left out of the side without any explanation.

'When I entered the dressing room at Goodison Park that night, Jimmy Adamson just walked past me,' Tony explains. 'There was nothing said, not a word, but the team was up on the wall, and I wasn't in it!

'I just couldn't believe it. We hadn't lost a game in weeks. I had come back into the side, picked up the captaincy again, and we were playing really well. The assistant manager, Dave Merrington, came up to me and apologised for the way it had been done, but Adamson didn't say a word to me. He couldn't look me in the eye.

'To make matters worse, obviously we lost the game,' Tony continues. 'It later became clear that we had been relegated as well. That was a big shock. We thought we were safe. I know Adamson thought we were safe.'

To add to the state of confusion that night, the radio announcer at Goodison Park had incorrectly given the final score from Highfield Road as Coventry City 2 Bristol City 1, a result that would have relegated the away side. But Sunderland fans, listening on transistor radios, knew differently and eventually the truth emerged.

'Adamson was just one of those guys where everything was about the youth system,' Tony says. 'He didn't go down too well with the senior players at Sunderland at all. I think they could see what was going to happen. Players like Bobby Kerr and Dick Malone were pushed out of the team a bit. He just totally believed in youth-team players. He did the same when he was manager of Burnley. They all wanted to play, and he had a hold over them, and that is the way it was.

'I tried to see him after the game, but he just ignored me and went straight to the press,' Tony adds. 'So I knew the writing was on the wall for me. I didn't go back to Sunderland on the team bus afterwards, I decided to go to Manchester instead, and stayed there for a couple of days before returning to the north-east.

'I never had a conversation with Adamson after it happened. There was nothing at all. I got a phone call from Jim Montgomery, who was at Birmingham City at the time, and he asked me if I would like to go down to St Andrew's for talks.

'I didn't want to leave Sunderland, but I could see what was happening. So, with the situation being what it was, and with me being in the England squad, and Birmingham being in the First Division, I went down to see them and I ended up signing for them.

'I didn't want to go,' Tony emphasises. 'Being at Sunderland was a nice time in my life and I enjoyed every minute of it. But it was just one of those things, and I think it came as a big surprise to some of the other players and the directors as well when it happened. But that is football and that is the way it goes sometimes.

'It was a shock to me, and I still believe that I didn't get the true story across to the Sunderland supporters. I don't think they realised what actually happened regarding me.

'Adamson wanted me out. It's as simple as that. I don't know why, because I was still only a young player myself at 25 years of age. I don't know if he thought I had too much influence in the dressing room? I just don't know.

'But I didn't want to leave and I really want to put that message out there in this book to all the Sunderland fans.

'Birmingham wasn't a professional set-up,' Tony continues. 'It was a bit lackadaisical, to be honest. Willie Bell signed me and then Sir Alf Ramsey took over. He was one of the club directors at the time and he came in on the understanding that he would have the full reins when it came to buying and selling players.

'He was a fantastic fellow, Alf. He would say to us, "Don't call me 'Boss' whatever you do, call me 'Sir Alf.'" He wanted to sell Trevor Francis and build a new team at Birmingham, but the board blocked it and that is why he left. About a year later Francis left anyway.'

Towers remained in the England squad for the early qualifying matches of the 1978 World Cup campaign. But he was never to be capped again, and after Don Revie controversially left to pursue a new managerial career in the United Arab Emirates there were to be no more call-ups. His time at Birmingham lasted for two seasons before he accepted an offer to play in the North American Soccer League with Montreal Manic.

'I will never forget when my son took a call at home from this agent in the US. He handed the phone to me and said, "Dad, there's a cowboy on the phone for you!" That was my introduction to the NASL! Gordon Hill, who I knew very well and who played out there, had passed on my number,' Tony says. 'It was a big move for us and a new way of life. The franchise was owned by Molson, the biggest brewery in the east of Canada, so there was a lot of backing for us. We played in the Olympic Stadium in Montreal, and we played in front of packed houses. We had first-class travel everywhere, and due to the huge distances and time zones, we always travelled at least 48 hours before a match.'

While Towers was there, Le Manic – as they were known by their fans – set a new record attendance of 58,542 in a play-off match against the Chicago Sting.

'It was a great,' Tony recalls. 'There was worldwide intrigue in the NASL at that time and that had a lot to do with the players it attracted. Pelé, Bobby Moore, Franz Beckenbauer, Johan Neeskens, Johan Cruyff were all out there. Cruyff said I finished him, by the way. He was playing for Washington, I made a tackle and he got carried off. I can't see it myself, but that is what he said to the press!

'There was actually a lot of pressure on us to perform and even though we had contracts, they weren't guaranteed. If it was felt that you weren't playing to your true ability, you could be out.

'I played against the best in the world, there were some true legends out there, and while it lasted it was a very exciting time. After the team in Montreal folded I played in the indoor league and then I went to Washington before Rodney Marsh took me over to Tampa Bay Rowdies. I had a season and half with him and then Vancouver Whitecaps came in for me.

'I think it could happen again over there,' Tony adds. 'Major League Soccer has much better players nowadays and it is big money, plus the crowds are better and the coverage is better. When I was there, TV wanted it, but the press didn't – I think they knew about American football, baseball, basketball, hockey and they didn't want to have to learn the rules!'

Towers returned to play in England in 1985 with two games for Vic Halom's Rochdale in the Fourth Division.

'I did Vic a favour,' Tony says. 'I was training up at Oldham with Joe Royle and Willie Donachie when he rang me up and asked me to help him out. I remember it was a particularly bad winter, and it was a shock to the system for me going there. I played a couple of games for him, and it was probably the worst thing I ever did in football, to be honest. But I was helping out a friend. I didn't get paid for it and I decided to finish my career there and then. I was only in my early thirties.'

Over 40 years on, I am sure that I still have a bubblegum card with Tony Towers' picture and name on it somewhere. He remains a hero to me, as I know he does to many other Sunderland fans of my generation, and he will always be a reminder of that glorious summer back in 1976 when, for albeit a very brief time, everything seemed as though it could be possible for us . . . I think it is known as the innocence of childhood. Eight relegations later, it certainly feels like that.

8

Stefan Schwarz brought the kind of quality to the Stadium of Light that has too often been lacking over the decades.

Here was a player who oozed class and composure but, unlike so many with that skill-set to have played for Sunderland since the Premier League era began, Stefan showed commitment too. He was the real deal in red and white where, regardless of a career spent at the top end of leagues across Europe, he bought into newly promoted Sunderland as a footballer, and might yet be involved in helping to buy into Sunderland once again.

Away from football, Schwarz may have had to agree not to travel into space, but somehow he always managed to find it when he was on the pitch. Should the Swede ever return in some capacity The Lads could have lift-off once again.

STEFAN SCHWARZ

MEETS GRAEME ANDERSON

Stefan Schwarz is not one for regrets – not after what has been achieved in a career spanning three decades, six top European leagues, World Cup appearances, league titles and cup finals. But, recalling how close Sunderland came to European football two seasons in a row between 2000 and 2002, elicits just a hint of wistfulness.

'It was a pity,' he says. 'It would have meant a lot to take Sunderland into Europe. Had we qualified I actually think our team would have done well – the way we were set up I think it would have suited us. It would have been an achievement on an unbelievable level from where the club had been just a short while previously, and excellent for Sunderland supporters too – they deserved it.

'We shouldn't think about what we didn't achieve, though, we should remember what was achieved because what was achieved was great.'

Schwarz is talking to me in the lounge bar of a hotel in Maida Vale, west London, and our conversation is being held in English, because multilingual, I'm not. I check how many languages Stefan is up to now.

'I speak six: English, Swedish, Italian, French, German, Portuguese,' he says. 'Seven if you include Mackem.'

The Swede had stayed over in the capital as a guest of former club Arsenal, where he is fondly remembered for his contribution to the Gunners' 1994-95 season, which included helping them to the UEFA Cup-Winners' Cup final. He is even more fondly remembered on Wearside, where he made just over 90 appearances for Sunderland from 1999–2003.

The vast majority of those games, however, came in just two seasons – the 1999-2000 and 2000-01 campaigns – when Sunderland were second in the league at Christmas and seventh at season's end on both occasions. For that reason he is always associated with the brief but golden era when the Black Cats showed they could go toe-to-toe with the Premier League's top dogs and hold their own.

It was to be Sunderland's most successful league spell since the 1950s, and it came just a handful of years after Sunderland were almost relegated to the third tier of the game, which made it all the more compelling to be part of. The club had come a long way in a short space of time under manager Peter Reid. But the signing of Schwarz on the eve of Sunderland's second shot at the Premier League was an acknowledgement the club needed to move into a different league in more ways than one. Reid knew that if his side were to genuinely prosper in the top flight they would need a touch of Continental class to supplement the British bulldog spirit upon which previous progress had been built. And Schwarz, who boasted a world-class pedigree, was the player Reid made his top summer target.

By this stage of Schwarz's career, the all-action midfielder was 30 years old, with a great career already behind him and the prospect of one final big move in front of him. He had won honours across the Continent with hometown club Malmö, Bayer Leverkusen, Benfica, Arsenal, Fiorentina and Valencia on his CV. He had played in World Cups and was a key part of the Swedish side which finished third in 1994, beaten only by eventual winners Brazil.

Sunderland was not a name you would naturally expect to appear next on his CV.

But after an epic pursuit, Schwarz was to become Sunderland's record signing when he eventually arrived in a £3.75 million deal from Valencia, dwarfing the previous £1.3 million record paid for Niall Quinn's services three years earlier.

Memorable now for the most celebrated contract clause in football history – an agreement that the player would not embark on space travel while at the Stadium of Light – negotiations took weeks to conclude and nervy Sunderland could never be sure they had their man until the very last moment.

Recalling that summer, Schwarz explains, 'I had been signed by Claudio Ranieri at Valencia but when he left and the new manager Héctor Cúper came in he wanted his own players, so I was free to look around.

'I'd had a good season with Valencia, scored some cracking goals, and I'd also played for Sweden against England at Wembley and against Liverpool in the UEFA Cup, and in both matches I had good games, so there was a lot of interest in me. I had many offers in England and also Europe – Portugal, Spain, Italy – then Liverpool came in. Gérard Houllier knew me from the international scene.

'But by then I liked the project at Sunderland and the way they had conducted themselves. I appreciated how hard they fought and worked to get me, and how Peter Reid presented the challenge.

'We spent a lot of time negotiating. It took quite a while forwards and backwards, but they were very understanding, and I cannot get away from the fact that, for me, it was a great decision: Sunderland was a very important part of my life. What appealed to me was that everyone was talking about Sunderland getting relegated, and I had been playing for teams that had been playing to win titles and trophies all my life. I thought it might be interesting.

'The chairman Bob Murray too, impressed us – me and my wife Ceu (pronounced Sue) were invited over to join him for a meal, and the agents at the table were pressing me to sign. After a while, my wife said, "No, this is all in the hands of the solicitors" and Bob agreed with her immediately saying, "Tonight there will be no talk of contracts", and there wasn't. That impressed me.

'I looked into the club, I did my research. I knew they were newly promoted, new stadium. I had heard about the atmosphere and the fans and it appealed to me, so I made the decision and it was fine, I never had cause to regret it. The players and the staff and the supporters all made me all feel very welcome.'

And that space clause?

'It came about when the talks were dragging on,' smiles Schwarz. 'We all wanted the deal to be done but there were a few clauses still to be sorted out. We were sat about, bored, in the Charlie Hurley Centre, and the James Bond film *Moonraker* was on. I said, "Wow, wouldn't it be great to go into space like that?" At which point the two agents in the room said they had pre-booked tickets on the first commercial space flights that were planned and I could have one if I signed!

'We shook on the deal but when the club heard about the flight they inserted a clause saying, "Stefan is not allowed to go into outer space while he is a Sunderland player!"'

It hardly mattered as Schwarz and Sunderland took off almost immediately in the Premier League, despite a false start in the first game, a 4-0 defeat at Chelsea.

'I didn't play that first match against Chelsea but I was there and people forget how good Gianfranco Zola was that day,' Schwarz points out. 'It was a heavy defeat but it was a wake-up call, and we took it the right way. We knew that if we were going to play in the Premier League it was going to be tough, and it was going to be of a higher standard. But we also knew we could do better, and we didn't let that game affect us. We got more determined rather than discouraged, and that said a lot about our character.'

Schwarz too was learning – something which had been a feature of his whole career, and which would continue at Sunderland where he was asked to play in an unfamiliar role.

'I've always been a positive person, no matter what the challenge,' he says. 'When I was at Malmö I played left-back and central midfield and learned the game; when I was at Fiorentina in Serie A I learned the extremely technical way they approached football, with little room for expression and so much meticulously planned – a lot of good players from outside Italy struggle with that. At Benfica I got used to the lovely passing style of play they had; but the season I played at Arsenal under George Graham, where they played a direct style of football, with the ball often bypassing the midfield . . . that was very different for me, but there were also ways in which, as a midfielder, you could adapt your game to help the team.'

At Sunderland Schwarz's challenge was how best to fit into a team dealing with the unexpected loss of winger Allan Johnston, whose superb partnership with Michael Gray down the left-flank had been such a feature of promotion.

The Swedish international could have been forgiven for saying it wasn't his problem. His was a name of European significance, his pedigree impeccable, and though time and knocks had stripped some of the box-to-box elements from his game, he remained a top-quality international midfielder. He had recently been instrumental in helping Sweden qualify for the Euro 2000 finals. And the summer he signed for Sunderland, the summer of 1999, he had received the Swedish *Guldbollen* (Golden Ball), the honour bestowed on the player rated Sweden's best that year – not bad going considering the opposition for the trophy included the likes of Freddie Ljungberg and Henrik Larsson.

In those circumstances, Schwarz might have felt entitled, especially after a record sum was paid for him, to insist Sunderland should play him in his preferred central midfield role and look to build a team around him. But, demonstrating the professionalism which typified his career and his willingness to put the team before ego, he slotted into the unusual role on the left of midfield, justifying it to himself as part of the learning process.

'Central midfield was always my favourite position,' he agreed. 'But my tactical knowledge on the field and my versatility could be used in different ways and, of course, my mentality is more about winning the games, about how to make it happen, than anything else. When you talk about top players and their skills, to me, the really great players make other players better – so if I could help my teammates play better, then I was prepared to compromise for the good of the team.'

Schwarz, in being asked to play out on the left, was effectively being asked to do what no other central midfielder could do as well. But, in the new system, Schwarz was often on the left-wing only in theory – in practice he was a central midfielder playing out toward the left. The Swede did not have the pace or trickery to be an out-and-out winger, but he could cover that area defensively, tucking inside whenever possible, and he could move out to the flank to support Mickey Gray's attacking runs from left-back, while also providing cover when the defender was further up the field. It meant that although Sunderland had lost the attacking brio of Johnston, they had gained the game-craft of Schwarz, who allowed Gray his attacking runs while providing more defensive cover than Johnston had previously done.

'It was not hard for me to suit the team,' Schwarz shrugs. 'I was versatile, and that was a bonus for the team and the manager, plus I love to win games, I love to please the manager, and I love to challenge myself. You know, sometimes it is good for you to be out of your comfort zone, to prove yourself. When I started my career I was a left-back. I played left-back, left-wing, left midfield, and you learn. But I was lucky with the Sunderland team I played in. Mickey Gray, for example, was great, a good runner, always going forward, and he helped me out in providing an outlet – but I was there to help him too and bring out the best in him. I never played left-back at Sunderland, but there were times when I did think I was playing there during games: "Hey, Mickey! Come back, Mickey!"' he laughs. 'But the great thing about that team was that the players were always trying to give each other an option. We could play beautiful football, but we could also play a very high-intensity game, be physical when we needed to be.'

For that, they had to credit the managerial brains of Peter Reid and Bobby Saxton, who ensured they paid attention to both the physical and mental demands of the game.

'Peter Reid and Bobby Saxton were great at knowing how to get the most out of us,' the Swede insists. 'It was a like an orange, where you look to squeeze the last drop of juice out of it – and not just the once: next week they would look to go back and squeeze every drop out once again. How did they do that? Well, they had the knowledge and the man-management, and they got the most out of us because they were very good at it, week-in, week-out – it's not always about the tactical and technical things, it's about management skills.

'At that level, football is very demanding – it's all about work-rate and commitment, focus and being competitive – so it's a skill, man-management, in keeping the balance right between fun and work; concentration and relaxation. But we knew when it was serious and we knew when we could have a laugh, and I think team spirit was such a big thing – there were great relationships between the players. We met up quite a lot after training, had a good time together, and we were like brothers – some were little brothers, some were older – but it was a good combination between every one of us.

'Of course, in training, we left that friendship back in the training room and got stuck into each other.

'But when I look back on that side, that time, I think us lucky to have a lot of leaders in the team, leaders who wanted success for the club.'

Guardian writer Louise Taylor once compared Sunderland in those two seasons to a Mini car being driven flat out down a motorway, the vehicle building up tremendous speed and momentum but inevitably doomed to eventually break down as bits started to fly off. That was the case with Sunderland in both those campaigns: second at Christmas but blowing up in the home straight and ending just outside the European places. Each time they should have strengthened in the January transfer window, but their Achilles heel was that the funds could not be found.

I covered Sunderland Football Club for 20 years for the *Sunderland Echo* and one of the great ironies for me during that time was that when the club didn't have great managers or great teams, they had plenty of money (the early years of Drumaville and Ellis Short); and when they did have a great manager and team, like those two top-flight seasons under Reid, they proved incapable of finding anywhere near enough in terms of funding. What might have been accomplished had one or two star signings been made at that time? It's a failing that Schwarz is prepared to acknowledge.

'If you are competing with Arsenal, Liverpool, Man United, Chelsea, the big teams, as we were, then, of course, the squad is not as big as theirs,' he says. 'And I think as well, at that time, that was the moment when Sunderland should have made the effort to invest, to get some top-quality players to improve the squad even more. Because, if you are second in the Premier League, then it's not so difficult to attract players. Not everyone has the character, maybe like me, or some of the other players who have come up to Sunderland when their options could have been Manchester or London. So it was vital that Sunderland attracted players when people were noticing them, when the club was second in the league. I think that was a mistake by the club that they did not, or were not able to do that.'

Schwarz was staying at Sunderland, though, regardless of the climate being much less inviting than those offered in the Italian, Spanish and Portuguese leagues; regardless of the area not offering the glittering attractions of the likes of London and Manchester. There was a rumour that Schwarz left Arsenal after only one season because his wife Ceu did not like the cold weather. It was something Sunderland's negotiating team might have been aware of and fearful of, given the climate is even cooler by the Wear than it is by the Thames. But Schwarz says that Arsenal rumour was always an oversimplification.

'There are cultural differences if you come from Portugal, so it was a bit difficult, but I was a young player – younger – [but by] Sunderland I was more mature. It was a different time at Arsenal. With Sunderland, we were ready and prepared for the move. Sunderland is a bit colder and windier but the people are so warm and friendly and that made a difference. To me, the people of the north-east are like southern European people in their mentality and character – they have time for you. They will stop you on the street and talk to you for half-an-hour, an hour, and talk to you about football. Arsenal was a bit of a culture shock, but George Graham was a fantastic manager and I liked him and learned a lot from that team.

'Because it was a little more direct, and I wanted to play a bit more football, it was a challenge for me, but then I learned to improve other aspects of my game. It meant I learned how to play in a different style and, of course, we went to the Cup-Winners' Cup and were unlucky to lose in the final. But always the key for me as a player was to see every situation as an opportunity in which to learn. When Fiorentina came into the picture and I left Arsenal to go there, Serie A was the best league in the world at the time, so it felt all round that it was the best solution. I enjoyed Italy but it was different – no private life, a lot of staying in hotels before during and after the games, and pre-seasons were all about living entirely for the football. Tactically, too, it was very demanding, technically and mentally. I've played with many, many great players around the world, but some find it very difficult to succeed in Italy because so much of your actions and movements on the pitch are dictated by the management and, mentally, it is very, very demanding. You have to have discipline, and everything is analysed by the supporters and the media, while in England and Spain there is more freedom off the pitch and a little more freedom on it to express yourself. It is a little more mechanical – robotic – in Italy but it has its merits, and you know that if you can succeed there you're likely to be able to succeed pretty much anywhere.

'At Sunderland we had our moves, we had our offensive organisation, we knew what we were going to do and we had a bit more freedom that way, and the emphasis was put on the understanding between players, like Niall Quinn and Kevin Phillips and others, and I liked that.'

Schwarz had that hallmark of all genuinely top players, the ability to instantly sense the movements and runs of those around him, and the ability to put the ball where it needed to be.

'When I looked at my players at Sunderland, my teammates, you look at what they are capable of, how they run, how they move, and then you work out where they want the ball – in front of them, which side of them, and so on – and you start to build a team character and understanding. It makes it so easy, though, when you have a really good relationship. It stays with you too. A couple of years ago I went down to a couple of the training pitches that we have in Portugal and I saw a guy running in the distance and, even though I couldn't make out who it was, I thought, "That's Kevin Phillips" simply because of the way he was running. I remembered. And, sure enough, it was Kev, out there for pre-season training – still looking really sharp and fit by the way!

'But these were the understandings that the management at Sunderland wanted to build in us, and it served us well in games, knowing how each other played and where they were going to be on the pitch.

'We were a very hard team but when we attacked we came with a lot of people, a lot of players, and one of my strong points I think was that I could read the game, I could see the situation. Quite often you can lose the ball high up the pitch, and I could read the situation where the danger was, and there were a lot of times you could regain the possession again because we had the right balance in the team and would get into the right position to recover. When we were attack-minded, if we had plenty of players up the pitch, it was a great thing because if we lost the ball we could quickly get it back while we still had plenty of players up the pitch.'

As we talk, the sound system in the Marriott's lounge bar is gently pushing out ambient beats, and it feels appropriate given Schwarz has settled into a rhythm in his reminiscences similar to the rhythm he used to demonstrate in his playing career. The Swede exuded a Zen-like control and calm as a player, even when he was throwing himself full-bloodedly into challenges – and it helped at Sunderland that he was happy off the pitch as well as on it.

'I lived in Darras Hall when I was at Sunderland and the scenery is beautiful in the north – Durham, Northumberland, the Lake District. When you had time on your hands it was great to get out into it and see so many beautiful sights,' he says. 'I was born in Malmö, where the weather is quite similar, and I was born by the sea, so it is nice to have it very close to you, as it is at Sunderland. Yes, it's colder than many other countries, but it means a lot to me to see the sea, to look out at it, and when I did that, it felt like home.'

Those last few sentences border on the poetic, the romantic, not something you'd expect to hear from the lips of a typical footballer, but then Schwarz was never typical. How many players are accomplished martial artists, for example?

'I've always like self-defence,' he says. 'Even as a youngster. And I studied Wing Chun, which is a form of kung fu.'

When I Google it later, the description reads, 'martial art specialising in close-range combat – it is known for being economical, direct and efficient.' I can't help smile at how appropriate that wording is, given Schwarz's style of play. He became a third brown belt grade, and used it as a means of escaping the pressures of football: 'One of the reasons I like it is because I do not find it demanding – you don't get tired or sweaty and a lot of it is the mental thing, the concentration, the discipline. It was like a form of relaxation for me, and it was good to have a hobby when I was playing. All the expectations from the supporters, the club, the media . . . there is a high demand and, of course, I took my job seriously.

'I always did my homework, preparing for myself, preparing for the team and learning about my opponent on the pitch. You see lots of videos of the team and the game-plans and strategy. You think about football [for] many, many hours of the day – it's intense, and so I think it is good to have times when you don't think about football at all, and Wing Chun was my hobby.'

While he loved his hobby, his passion was his job, and he rarely enjoyed it more in any time of his career than those opening couple of seasons which reinforced in his own mind how much he had made the right decision in moving to Wearside.

'Playing at the Stadium of Light . . . oh, the games, they were unbelievable,' he murmurs, almost misty-eyed. 'It was amazing. Two or three hours before the game I got there and the first few times, when I saw people turning up, everyone in their red and white shirts – children, men, ladies, old people, everyone wearing red and white – I couldn't believe it. They reminded me of ants because everyone was moving around so busily and colourfully, and they all looked and dressed the same. I was so impressed I thought, "Wow, these people really love their club."

'And I liked the stadium too, a beautiful ground, with the supporters there greeting you. And you go down into the dressing room, and then you stand in the tunnel and you hear the classical music, and as you came out it turned into rock music – it made the hairs on the back of your neck stand on end. It made you feel twice as tall, the noise; the atmosphere was fabulous.'

Not only did Schwarz immediately buy into the Sunderland matchday experience, he also bought into the Sunderland psyche.

'You have to understand the people, you have to understand Sunderland fans if you are to play for them,' he insists. 'What are they, by and large? They are decent, honest, hard-working people who don't expect anything less than 100 per cent from you because if they were in your position they wouldn't give less than 100 per cent. They want you to give everything and, at that time, that's what we did from the start of the game. We would try to do it every match to get the crowd with us, to get the atmosphere behind us.

'Sunderland fans want to like their footballers because the club is the number one thing for them. So for me it is simple: all you have to do is give 100 per cent – it doesn't matter if you're not having a good day, as long as you're giving your best.

'You felt a lot of responsibility and you had to perform. You couldn't let them down, you couldn't complain about anything, you had to do the business.'

'Do the business': Sunderland certainly did, more often than not in those two seasons, helped by the fact that they were a well-oiled machine.

'We had the capacity to see games through very forcefully,' suggests Schwarz, with a hint of understatement. 'We knew no teams wanted to come to the Stadium of Light, no teams wanted to play against us. First of all, we had an excellent team, but we were so hard-working, so hard to beat. I think sometimes we would be playing teams there and you could almost sense them looking up at the clock after five minutes as if to think, "Oh my God, there's still 85 minutes to go!" That mental thing we had, where we had our opponents in our pockets and it was finished because they just wanted to go back home, that's because we could play good football but we also liked the physical side of it too. We were very competitive. There were some games when it felt like even though it was a flat pitch, we were playing downhill and our opponents were playing uphill because of the supporters. That's what they wanted straight away – complete commitment – and we could dictate the game, make it slower or quicken it up; and then you could get tactical as well: it was a really enjoyable team to be part of.

'If you look at our players, we were not nasty or dirty, we were honest. If you look at how we played, with that intensity, we respected each other and respected our opponents and took it seriously.'

Newly promoted Sunderland were the surprise package of the 1999-2000 campaign, quickly rising up the table on the back of good results – winning six of their seven league games during the months of September and October and drawing the other. And while every player played their part, much of their success was based on Reid's summer transfer work, and in particular with the acquisition of Schwarz and his former Arsenal teammate Steve Bould.

Peter Reid's 105-point championship-winning team had been built largely on the abundant energy and enterprise of youth but, upon reaching the top flight as a Sunderland manager for the second time, he knew the value of experience – that was a lesson learned from the Black Cats' previous relegation. With Bould, Schwarz and Niall Quinn, the side had strength and know-how running all the way through it, and the likes of Gavin McCann, Alex Rae and Kevin Ball in central midfield thrived on that.

'Steve Bould's knowledge about the game and the respect he had from opponents was special,' says Schwarz. 'He had played for Arsenal for many, many years. He had perfect experience, and the experience we had in the side from the senior players meant no one was overawed at being at this level.'

Schwarz is modest about his own contribution, but the calm authority and presence he exuded on the pitch also proved invaluable during those stellar campaigns. The Swede may have lost a yard or two of pace from his earlier days but what he brought to the side was ball-retention, composure and the ability to continually find a teammate with a pass. He could anticipate threats before they became dangerous and he was perfectly suited to Sunderland's style of never allowing the opposition to settle and always looking to make a tackle. In many ways he was like Paul Bracewell before him at Sunderland – tough as teak, never defeatist and a figure of reassurance when the side was under pressure.

There was no better example of Sunderland's growing confidence than the game which Schwarz credits as the best team performance he played in at the Stadium of Light: the 4-1 win over Chelsea in December 1999. In fact, that match and the 4-2 victory over Chelsea at Stamford Bridge the following season he regards as among his two most enjoyable games for the Black Cats.

'I played the full 90 minutes of the 4-1 win,' he remembers. 'And it was a privilege to be a part of it.

'The atmosphere was electric from the start because it was one of those games where we were out of the blocks from the whistle. And you have to remember who was in the Chelsea side: Marcel Desailly, a World Cup winner who could not live with Niall Quinn that day; and world-class players like Gustavo Poyet and Zola as well as fantastic competitors like John Terry and Dennis Wise. We totally dominated them and that first half in particular – when we went in 4-0 at half-time – was far and away the best 45 minutes' football from a team I was involved in during my time at Sunderland, and that's bearing in mind we had many good displays during that time.

'We had Chelsea as well at Stamford Bridge in March the following year, which people don't talk about quite so much, but which was a memorable game, possibly because my former boss Claudio Ranieri had taken over that season. I remember Ranieri catching up with me in the corridor outside the Chelsea changing rooms afterwards and shouting, "HOW DO YOU TRAIN!!!??" because he could not believe the intensity of our game.

'Looking back on those two seasons where we were in Champions League positions at Christmas and seventh at the end, they were incredibly similar, despite many players coming and going. We tried to improve but the big teams always invested a lot more and that always made it a challenge. A lot of people who thought we were a half-season wonder then changed that to a one-season wonder, they never thought we would do it two seasons in a row. They thought we had lost the element of surprise, but we showed we could do it in consecutive seasons, and to be second twice at Christmas showed a lot of quality in the team.'

Over the seasons, Schwarz also contributed the occasional goal to the cause.

'Three goals,' he smiles: 'Sheffield Wednesday, Arsenal and Ipswich Town. The one which stays in my mind, though, is probably the Arsenal one, even though the Sheffield Wednesday one was a great goal and a match-winner. Arsenal was the top corner from the edge of the penalty area. I took it on one foot, up in the air, and volleyed it home with the other from Nicky Summerbee's cross.

'Come to think of it, Sheffield Wednesday was a volley too – a cross from the right, volley.

'But I remember the Arsenal game because we were away from home and we played well and it was a beautiful goal, even if it was against my former club. We got a draw, but the quality of that Arsenal team we were playing . . . Henry, Ljungberg, Vieira! And the same went for the Man United and Chelsea teams – we held our own and won games against some great sides.'

There were many memorable wins over the lesser sides of the division too: the 5-0 crushing of Derby County for one, in mid-September 1999, which first signalled that Sunderland were going to be the real deal in the Premier League that time around.

'We won by a big margin but they actually played quite well, Derby,' says Schwarz. 'We were just very efficient in front of goal: everything we hit went in. To win by five, away from home, is never easy, but Kevin Phillips got a hat-trick that day, Niall Quinn got on the scoresheet and, if you look at so many of the good times, the goals from Quinn and Phillips are the common thread running through them. Kevin and Niall were so good, but they worked for the team and we were very happy to provide them with chances to score goals – and they were the sort of characters who, if they weren't getting chances, they would not sulk but go out there and create them themselves. They were great at creating space too. I would say Kevin Phillips, Ian Wright and Gabriel Batistuta were the three best strikers I played with in my career, and I played with a lot of top-class strikers.

'I normally put Batistuta out there in front, but Phillips is up there with the very best. With strikers like them, I usually sum it up saying if you gave them one opportunity, they'd score two goals! With those type of strikers, it is all about determination and conviction. They are very cold, very confident and, even if anything is in front of them – goalkeepers, defenders; anything – the ball will go into the net because they commit themselves totally. They have a total belief: they don't shoot because they hope they're going to score, they shoot because they know they're going to score.'

The strike pairing's contributions were rarely better highlighted than in the derby games and in particular the first back in the Premier League, which Sunderland won 2-1 in a biblical downpour at St James' Park in August 1999.

'The Newcastle games were always something special,' Schwarz smiles. 'Of course, I've played in many derbies over my career but the north-east derby was wonderful. Those games were all about character and personality and determination, and to win the game you needed to play at your highest level. It's a lot of emotion, a lot of determination, but it's also important in these games that you show patience and intelligence, to be cool, because it is very important to think clearly. Of course, there are moments when it is very physical, very demanding mentally, and with the two teams and the two clubs you have to understand what it means to play against each other. There's a lot of talk for a long time before and a long time afterwards, and I had the privilege to play in some great ones, the 1-2 in the rain, especially.

'The rain was incredible, the pitch was not in the best condition, but I think that the level of commitment, the passion and the goals we scored was something special. Niall was fantastic for us that night, and I'll always remember the way Kevin swivelled to smash home the winner: a goal from a natural goalscorer, it was like a film script.

'There was one when we were 2-0 down at the Stadium of Light, got it back to 2-2 and we should have won it – a great game.

'I remember Bobby Saxton in the dressing room beforehand saying the biggest cheer on the day will not be for the first goal but for the first big tackle, and I had a good one straight away, a very fair one, on Shearer right at the start of the game. It was a proper derby-type tackle, where we both went in hard for the ball and I remember the stadium was literally buzzing for a couple of minutes afterwards, you could feel it.

'Great games, and a pleasure to play in.'

These were immortal moments, but mortality was just around the corner for a player the wrong side of 30 whose game had involved constant challenges and hard tackling.

The mind remained willing but the body was not indestructible. And despite a phenomenal work ethic, Schwarz's two remaining seasons at Sunderland were affected by injuries and the management's fear he no longer had the legs to get around the pitch in the way the Premier League demanded.

I remember Peter Reid and Adrian Heath marvelling at Schwarz's chiselled physique when he returned to pre-season training for the ill-fated 2002-03 campaign. 'He's gone again,' they said in admiration. 'He's taken his condition to an even higher level, he's in amazing physical shape.' But their doubts persisted about how long he could continue at that level.

Schwarz had suffered a career-threatening Achilles injury in March 2000 which brought his debut Sunderland season to a premature end and might even have affected the Black Cats' chances of qualifying for Europe that season.

He also missed the start of the following season as a result of the injury, not returning to the side until the start of December and a 2-0 win over Everton.

His prolonged absence from club football persuaded him to retire from the international game. He had been capped 69 times and could have had many more, but it was the second time he had been injured in an international shirt while on the Black Cats' books.

'Reidy was understanding about the injury and he said these things happen,' recalls Schwarz. 'But I wasn't happy because I wanted to play for my club, Sunderland, my employer. I loved the place and I wanted to play week in week out, especially when I felt so welcomed by the team and the city. It was a very frustrating time for me. It was a pity, but that was why I gave up international football and retired – I did it for Sunderland Football Club.'

Schwarz pushed himself and returned, but it became harder for him to nail down a regular place in the starting line-up. He made 20 appearances in the 2001-02 campaign in which relegation was narrowly avoided but, with injuries continuing to mount, he made just two appearances (both in the League Cup) in the 2002-03 season, which saw Sunderland relegated with just 19 points.

Schwarz had decisions to make on his future.

'Of course, as a professional footballer you are rarely 100 per cent when you are playing,' he says. 'But I started to feel it a little bit in the knee when changing direction. You can use painkillers for the games, that's fine, but then you have the training during the weeks as well, and I train just the same as I play. That was a challenge.'

Facing the end of his Sunderland career, Schwarz had options.

'I could probably have played at a lower level,' he says. 'I could have adapted my game. I got an offer from Saudi Arabia – a lot of money – and I thought about it. But it was that time the US was heavily involved in Iraq, so it wasn't the best part of the world to be in! Sunderland had offered me a coaching job, but I had played at the highest levels in European competition so it didn't really appeal to me, and then my son was diagnosed with autism, and it was a very dark time for us. He didn't speak for six years, he would keep away from people, and I wanted to concentrate on him 24/7 at that time. I decided to retire because it was not good for me to be far away from my family any longer. It was the right thing to do generally and the right thing to do for my wife and family. I had my football as an outlet in my life but Ceu didn't, and it was unfair to leave her to cope with the challenge.'

Thankfully, Mr and Mrs Schwarz's hard work was rewarded. Their son Jürgen is now 21 and has come far since his early days.

'He now speaks two languages,' beams Schwarz, 'and we are so proud of the way he was able to develop.'

The midfielder's dwindling influence over the course of his time on Wearside also coincided with Sunderland's own decline as a footballing force.

'We started to decline simply because key players got injured or left the club and it proved hard to replace them,' says Schwarz, without any trace of doubt. 'It's important to have leaders on the pitch, which we had, and we played well together and had a good understanding. But sometimes when players start to lose games, start to lose a little bit, they're not mentally strong. So it's very important you have players who can show the way when you're in a tough moment, when you don't get results and the fans are not happy and it is not great in the media.

'Unfortunately for us, we lost some of those players who could have coped when the difficult times came.'

If you prompt many of the players who transitioned from the Roker Park to the Stadium of Light era, they will quietly suggest that the increase in foreign players was what ultimately led to Sunderland's Premier League demise. With the cost of home grown talent too pricey for the Black Cats' limited coffers, Peter Reid was forced to look abroad and, over the course of time, team spirit was diluted by players who didn't share the same natural commitment to the club's cause, or struggled to acclimatise to language or culture.

But, whenever that theory is advanced, Schwarz is always a foreign player who is excluded from criticism.

Home-grown players recognised that although the Swede was different from them in many ways, he shared the same desire to put his body on the line and desperation to win games. For Schwarz, it was more about the content of a player's character rather than the colour of their skin or their country of birth.

'Kevin Ball was a huge influence around the club, but he and Steve Bould were gone by the end of my first season,' says Schwarz. 'Alex Rae went, and Don Hutchison too, and then we had injuries. I was out for more than six months and, crucially, Niall Quinn started to struggle with them.

'It's about character and mentality. I've played in front of huge crowds, and you need to handle it. If you don't have players who can do that, you can soon be in trouble.'

Relegation and the final break-up of the team he had graced hurt Schwarz because he had come to identify so much with the club.

He still does, 'Sunderland are Premier League in every aspect: the stadium, the training facility, the supporters – and it hurt me then to see them go into the Championship, just as it hurts me now to see them back in the Championship again. You always want to bounce back straight away, but maybe this time it will take two or three seasons. All I know is that it is a club that deserves to be in the Premier League. It may be that it takes a lot of money for that to happen, but I think it is a club that should be of interest to investors because the club has a lot of ingredients for success.'

That last sentence was offered not without a degree of self-interest from the Swede: he is, after all, one of the best-connected men in football, with a string of important and influential contacts across the Continent. He was linked over the summer of 2017 with a consortium interested in buying the club from Ellis Short and, while the American held on to the club in the end, you would not bet against Schwarz returning to Sunderland in some capacity one day. He is so well connected in the world of football – as much at home in the boardroom as he is in the dressing room – that you could envisage him at ease as manager, chairman or director of football. Certainly, Sunderland remains close to his heart, and he's as well positioned as anyone to understand the potential of a club that few outside the area genuinely grasp.

When his former teammate Niall Quinn retired as a player, chairman Bob Murray told the Irishman he wouldn't be surprised if one day he returned as Sunderland manager. 'Don't be surprised if I come back as chairman!' Quinn famously retorted, and several years later did just that.

Schwarz too is someone whose playing days at Sunderland might not spell the end of his connection with the red and whites. Who knows, maybe one day he will fulfil that dream of taking the club into Europe, after all.

Sunderland fans can dream.

9

Vic Halom was the cult hero's cult hero. In an age when defenders could just about chop opponents in half and count themselves unfortunate to get a booking, Halom was having none of that. He was a centre-forward who liked to get his retaliation in first! Vic took no prisoners on the pitch yet always played with a smile, a touch of devilment and plenty of humour as he played up to the crowd. He also scored some great and important goals, which is what matters most if you lead the line.

Halom was the front man as Sunderland won the FA Cup in 1973. That alone would have been sufficient for him to pass into legend but over and above that achievement Vic embodied the spirit that Sunderland supporters desire in anyone who pulls on the stripes. Now in his late sixties, Vic has left his home in Bulgaria to come and live in Sunderland.

VIC HALOM

MEETS ROB MASON

Eleven talented footballers do not necessarily equate to a great team. There has to be the right blend. The 1973 Cup winners, like the promotion winners of 1964, became lifelong friends, brothers in arms. These are players who shared an experience so deep that it defined their careers. Whatever else they achieved – even for Dave Watson, who went on to play 65 times for England; or Dennis Tueart, who starred for Manchester City and was signed by New York Cosmos as Pelé's replacement – it is the fact that they were Stokoe's Stars who won the most sensational of FA Cup finals that carves their names into red and white history.

Only one goal was scored in that final. Scorer Ian Porterfield earned world renown on the back of it, going on to manage in Africa, Asia and the Caribbean as well as Britain. 'Porter' was a terrific player and a deserving hero but 'YouTube' the Cup-final goal and you'll see how close he came to not being the cup-winning goal scorer.

As Billy Hughes's corner floats in from the left-hand side, the Leeds defence are distracted by the figure of Dave Watson. Centre-forward Vic Halom is first to the ball and, having knocked it down, looks as if he's favourite to reach it and score himself before Porterfield strikes. Is that how Vic sees it? 'Yes. I'd actually knocked it down for myself and when Porter hit it I struggled to get out of the way. The ball dropped, it came up off my shin and I was ready to volley it but Ian was there.'

Who knows what might have happened had Halom connected? The net might have bulged, with Vic the name in lights on the scoreboard – or maybe his effort might have been blocked or gone wide. 'Ian was closer and facing the right way so I had to get out of the way,' recalls Vic, who was nothing short of a brilliant centre-forward for Sunderland. In my 50-plus years of watching Sunderland only Niall Quinn rivals Vic for a place in the best XI I've seen. Equally, only Vic rivals Quinny among players when it comes to being the biggest character.

The remainder of the cup-winning team were already at the club when Halom was signed. Although he had played for Bob Stokoe earlier in his career, Vic wasn't part of the Messiah's master plan. However, with Dave Watson having been converted to a centre-half, Sunderland needed a centre-forward.

Billy Hughes's brother John had been signed. A Scotland international who won six league titles and five cups with Celtic, 'Yogi' had also played in the 1970 European Cup final. Five years older than Billy, John Hughes joined Sunderland in January 1973 only to suffer what would be a career-ending injury on his debut against Millwall at Roker Park. Had he not been injured Sunderland almost certainly would not have signed Halom and almost certainly would not have gone on to win the FA Cup. Quite apart from Halom's contribution, John Hughes was cup-tied having played in the third round for Crystal Palace.

'John was still around when I came to Sunderland,' explains Vic. 'In fact, we bought his house at Oxclose in Washington, but I think that was only after the decision had been made that he wasn't going to be able to play again. He never trained. He was a big fella. He was bigger than me and twice as quick – and that's not difficult. When he hit you, you would stay hit.'

So often in Sunderland's subsequent history fate has conspired to deny them. However, when Halom arrived to complete a side about to become known as Stokoe's Stars circumstances dictated that Sunderland's name was written on the cup long before they even got to Wembley.

A couple of weeks after Stokoe's arrival a flu epidemic intervened to leave The Lads without a game for three weeks, giving the new manager a chance to take stock of his charges. When play resumed bottom-of-the-table Brighton pitched up at Roker Park minus their regular keeper Brian Powney as Sunderland strode to their biggest win of the season.

The following home league game, against Millwall, brought victory, the injury to John Hughes and the subsequent signing of Hallom. Vic would debut in the next league match at Sheffield Wednesday, the scene of his goal in the FA Cup semi-final two months later. Whatever mishaps hit Sunderland, under the Messiah of Bob Stokoe water was turned into wine.

'I don't know whether it was ordained or not,' ponders Vic. 'A few weeks earlier I had played at Roker Park against Sunderland. I never really thought much of it. It was just another game. I had scored and we'd won.' Halom's header had helped Luton to win on Wearside in the league in the month before Stokoe took over. Vic had been in typical form off the pitch as well as on it: 'I remember afterwards Bob Cass the reporter saw me and said, "That's what a footballer should look like" – because I'd got a beer in one hand and a cigarette in the other.'

Once he started playing for Sunderland rather than against them Vic had no problems settling in. The Black Bush numbered among Halom's haunts as he lived life to the full, just as there were no half measures when it came to putting in a shift in a match: 'I always had a pint with the lads. Now I go to the Jolly [Sailor] in Whitburn. We have some great nights, just talking and having a laugh. The thing about Sunderland, and the reason I decided to come back here, is because of the humour. They have a sense of humour over everything. People like to laugh here.

'Billy and Big John [Hughes] would come down and we'd spend Sundays at the Boilermakers' Club. We'd have a couple of beers on a Sunday lunchtime and they'd have some acts on. I remember Cannon and Ball were on there. They walked off the stage because nobody was listening to them. They had these poor strippers on, which nobody even looked at because everyone was playing dominoes! That was my best sport – fives and threes – brilliant.'

Footballers were big stars in the early seventies but it was nothing like today, when the most bog-standard player can often live a life that is light years away from the people supporting them. Shielded by security guards and press officers a player's connection with the public is frequently frozen into time-allotted slots where the two might come together at an organised event. Don't expect to run into a trio of Sunderland players playing doms in your local 'workies' any time soon.

When the FA Cup was won under Stokoe there were three moments that stood out: from the final, Porterfield's goal and Monty's miraculous double save; and from the cup run Vic Halom's goal against Manchester City. The fifth-round replay against City was voted the 'Match of the Century' when Roker Park closed 24 years later.

What is generally considered the greatest ever World Cup final had taken place three years earlier. The last goal as Brazil beat Italy 4-1 in Mexico, was a work of art as the ball was worked across the edge of the Italian box for Pelé to lay the final pass into the path of Carlos Alberto – later a teammate of Dennis Tueart in New York. Halom's goal that put Sunderland 1-0 up as FA Cup favourites City were beaten 3-1 was arguably even better because Vic's finish was from a more difficult angle. It was a very similar goal as the ball was worked from left to right across the edge of the box with a series of slick passes and intuitive movement.

As Bobby Kerr slipped a cute, angled pass into the path of Halom at the Fulwell End it was Vic's fourth game for the club and only the second time home fans had seen him in Sunderland colours. It is a goal he has talked about thousands of times. It is the moment that secured his place in red and white folklore. He may well have a stock answer when asked about it – a bit like Paul McCartney being asked about how he came to write 'Yesterday' – but can Vic actually visualise the moment in his memory rather than recollecting it from so many TV re-runs? 'It's framed in my mind because it was special. It was special because it went on to become historic. I've scored a lot of goals from a lot of angles and a lot of distances – overhead kicks, all sorts. I had ability. You were taught by Stokoe not to overdo it: "Don't fanny around with the ball. Don't do this or that. Get it and go, Get it and go!" You had to do that or you'd get flattened! In that sense, when the ball has come to me, the work that had been put in by Porter and little Bobby and co. It just lifted a little bit and I smacked it. The funniest thing was Joe Corrigan shouted, "Leave it" and it went "*zuump*!" right in the corner of the net and Franny Lee went up to him and said, "Leave it? What do you bloody mean "Leave it?" – or something like that, there was a fair bit of swearing!

'When I'd played for Luton at Sunderland there were less than 15,000 people watching. People had lost a little bit of faith. What the players were able to demonstrate once they were given the freedom to go and play was that they had an enormous amount of talent that had been choked. You had Billy, Dennis, Bobby, Ian and so on. They just blossomed. I mean this. We played against some of the top teams in Europe, certainly some of the top teams in England, and they weren't a patch on us. Not a patch! Arsenal? We cruised it. It wasn't even tough. I've been in a lot tougher games than that. Man City? They were big clubs and we destroyed them because the players had got this belief in themselves as a team. The work-rate was fabulous and the ability was there. It is very difficult to play at that pace. Nobody was wandering around pussyfooting with one-twos and that. It was done at top speed, with a lot of effort and accuracy. I loved it as a centre-forward. I'd had a little ex-Celtic winger at Leyton Orient who would just stick it in front of you. He wouldn't bother taking on the full-back all the time. He'd just look up and stick it in front of you. Bobby did exactly the same. He'd get a little bit of space and put the ball where it was dangerous. Ian did the same, and then you had the runners and they had real ability. Hughesy scored some fabulous goals. The amount of ability that was in that team was phenomenal. The amount of sheer effort Bobby and Ian put in was matched by everyone. Billy and Dennis worked as hard as everyone else and, of course, once they got the ball they had the ability to make the most of it.

'The quality within our team was mind-blowing and the work ethic was there to complement it. Not only could we play but we really did work hard. We knew that if you put people under pressure they made mistakes.

'The atmosphere within the camp was player-driven. It was great. We had Arthur Cox there. Arthur was a little regimental. Sometimes we took notice of him and sometimes we didn't because we had a good time. The preparation was there. Once we'd done the work we wanted to have a laugh. What disappointed me no end was when the government brought in a no-pay-rise policy and the lads who weren't being paid an awful lot of money – and they had earned it – were tempted away by a decent wage. I wish that had never happened.'

The cup-winning team broke up too quickly after the Wembley success. Injury cruelly ended Ritchie Pitt's playing days, while 10 months to the day after the cup final, Dennis Tueart scored twice in what would be his final appearance before joining Manchester City along with Micky Horswill. As the pair left for Manchester, cup-holders Sunderland were a modest 10th in the Second Division. It was a season where Halom's 21 goals made him top scorer in a year when the players had to cope with every team raising their game against the side that had become the first Second Division outfit in 41 years to win the FA Cup.

'Teams did raise their game every week,' remembers Vic, 'and we found that as tough as anything. The concentration had gone and the effort wasn't at the same level because there were ulterior motives driving players. I regret that, and it could have been handled better. They were all local lads. They had been taught the business and they had the ability.'

Back in 1973 play-offs were well over a decade away. Had they been in existence then, with the momentum and belief Stokoe's Stars possessed, there was every likelihood Sunderland would have won promotion too. 'I think we would have won any play-offs,' states Vic, adding, 'I think when I signed we were near the bottom.'

Halom had come into a team in 17th position, two places higher than when Stokoe took over. Despite winning only one of the last five league games (the focus being on the final), Sunderland finished sixth, which would have taken them into any play-offs. In 1973-74, while the FA Cup team was still intact bar the injury-stricken Pitt, Sunderland were drawn against Derby County in the League Cup. It was a competition undertaken far more competitively than now. After two pulsating meetings, a second replay was won 3-0 courtesy of a Halom hat-trick. 'When we were 2-0 ahead, Dennis opened them up and gave me a tap-in for the hat-trick,' he recalls. Those goals were netted against a club who had finished seventh midway through a spell when they won the title twice in four years with a back four of England defenders in David Nish, Colin Todd, Roy McFarland

and Henry Newton, alongside Ron Webster, who was voted the club's best ever right-back.

Halom's previous cup goal had come in the semi-final of the FA Cup against Arsenal. While the other goal Vic netted in the cup run was that blistering shot against Manchester City, his opening goal against the Gunners was of an earthier nature. Nineteen minutes into the game Micky Horswill played a ball over the top. Arsenal centre-half Jeff Blockley wasn't just favourite to reach it first, Halom had no right to get anywhere near it but sped after the defender who tickled it back towards his keeper Bob Wilson. Chasing everything with the determination that epitomised the cup run, Halom got there a split second before Wilson, knocked it past him and bundled the ball into an empty net.

Where the picture-book strike against Manchester City is etched into Halom's memory, and he can recall knocking the ball beyond Wilson at Hillsborough, the recollection of the beginning of his semi-final goal is somewhat cloudier: 'I can't remember the distances but, again, a lot of what you did, didn't pay off. There were one or two efforts in that game where I felt I should have scored, but if you don't put the effort in you can't get the rewards.'

Arsenal had been bidding to become the first club to reach three consecutive FA Cup finals since Blackburn Rovers in the 1880s and fell behind to a goal from a man who could have been playing for them. 'When I was at Leyton Orient, Arsenal had made an offer for me,' explains Vic. 'The way I understood it was they offered a young Charlie George and twenty grand for me. Jimmy Bloomfield turned it down. My dad had letters saying Arsenal wanted me but Leyton Orient wanted too much money.'

Contemplating his goal in the semi-final, Halom continues, 'That's all inside your head, so whenever I was playing a team who wanted me it provided an extra dimension. Not because

I wanted to go to Arsenal but because they had expressed an interest in me. I didn't know who Jeff Blockley was. Their normal centre-half was Frank McLintock but he was sat in the stand. Now Frank's a different kettle of fish, but you chase everything down and put pressure on defenders and goalkeepers. That's why I did it. If they make a mistake you're in.'

Having scored in the key fifth-round replay and the semi-final, quite apart from getting out of the way as Porterfield plundered the cup-winning strike from Vic's knock-down, Halom did have the ball in the net at Wembley. As well as forcing Leeds' keeper David Harvey into his best save of the final with a shot from the edge of the box two minutes from time, Vic bundled Harvey and the ball over the line only for it to be disallowed. 'I think they should have given it,' Vic laughs. These days he'd get a card for such a challenge but in a bygone era it would have stood – certainly Nat Lofthouse's challenge on Harry Gregg for Bolton's second goal in the 1958 final against Manchester United was even more robust than Halom's on Harvey.

Had Sunderland not won the FA Cup that moment might have been more of a talking point, but there was to be no debate: the cup was won, and deservedly so. 'The principle stayed the same whenever we played – and especially in that game,' reflects Vic. 'Our team was made up of good players. Take nothing away from them, they were top, top players. We were playing Leeds, who were top class. In order to combat that, Micky, Billy, Bobby, Dennis and Porter – their work-rate was unreal. For Micky, as the youngest member of the side, to perform as he did against such quality was out of this world. The back four of Dick, Dave, Ritchie and Guth – I thought were absolutely fabulous, but that's because they were put under a lot of pressure. I still laugh whenever I see Ritchie's first-minute tackle on Allan Clarke! They coped well and withstood it all, and then there was Monty and his heroics. That defensive system was excellent and the more I watch that game the more I appreciate it. For me up there I had a job to do against their defenders, so all I could do was try to get a bite in, so I spent most of the game running, just chasing things. That's why I had cramp. I'd never had cramp in my life, but on that surface I did more running than ever and hardly touched the ball – but part of the team's principles was work-rate, work-rate, work-rate. It was staggering, really, and with a little bit of luck we could have won by a bigger margin.'

If a goalkeeper is the first line of attack as well as the last line of defence – as exemplified by Jordan Pickford – then a centre-forward can also be the first line of defence. That is not to say a striker can just be a workhorse – he needs to get his share of goals as well – but if a team have a number nine putting a shift in it sets the right tone for the rest of the side, who can see the front man grafting. Halom was a defender's worst nightmare because he was a threat with and without the ball. With the ball he was a threat to the goal. Without the ball he was a threat to the defender.

In football, you can coach technique but you can't coach heart. You either have it or you don't. Lee Cattermole has it, Kevin Ball had it. You don't need to be a destroyer to have heart – look at Julio Arca. Vic Halom was as tough as they come, and remember he was playing in an era when you had to be hard. What made Vic especially teak-tough? Where did that inner strength come from?

Born in 1948, three years after the end of the Second World War, Halom is as straightforward about his upbringing as he was on the pitch. He explains, 'I was being carried by my mum when they came to England. My dad had escaped from Hungary and my mum had escaped from Germany.' During the FA Cup run stories emerged about a possible call up by

Hungary for Burton-on-Trent lad Halom, whose family story is a fascinating tale: 'My dad played football and he wasn't bad. He was a left-back. He'd been playing for the Austrian police team in their area and had got a toe injury. He had to go to hospital, and that's where he met my mum, who was a nurse.

'They managed to get a passage over to England. In those days they were given the options of working on the land or down the pit. My dad went down the pit. He trained somewhere in Lancashire and then came down to South Derbyshire and worked at Granville Colliery for a good while before the pits amalgamated and he became a shot-firer at Rawdon Colliery.'

Sunderland's FA Cup-final team consisted of six north-easterners (including sub David Young, plus manager Bob Stokoe), four Scots and two men from the Midlands, Notts-born Dave Watson and Derbyshire lad Halom. In the modern era teams would be expected to have numerous players from around the world, but in the Team of '73 Halom's background made him the closest thing to exotica. Indeed Vic didn't start to speak English until he went to school: 'My first language was German. My dad was Hungarian and nobody other than Hungarians speak Hungarian. My mum spoke Russian because of her background. On her side, my grandad was an officer who was killed by the Red Army. They lived in the Ukraine.'

The story widens as Vic's trail of ancestry leaves him looking like an ideal subject for the genealogy TV series, *Who Do You Think You Are?*: 'I've found out that it is very difficult to track down but it is something that I feel very strongly about. My mum, especially, warned me off and told me not to go into it. All I know was there was the White Army and the Red Army. My grandmother had passed away at an early age with a heart problem, and so my mum was moved to her nearest relative, who was an aunt in Germany, as far as I was told.

'From there my mum escaped into Austria with a friend and some other people who were doing the same thing. She and her friend Emma were thrown over the wire on the border and landed in Austria, but men were shot on the wire. My mum was called Renata Berja, but in England she called herself Ida. My dad was Louis or "Lajos", as it was pronounced [Vic's middle name is Lewis]. His brothers joined him in 1956 after the Hungarian uprising. We were always steered away from the history. My mum and dad spoke German at home so I only spoke German when I turned up for my first day at school. Every other five-year-old had to learn English as well as me, so it wasn't a problem.'

Coincidentally, when the Hungarian uprising began in October 1956 the youth team of Hungary played England at Roker Park, and, as Vic will explain, his dad later had a role to play for his home nation at Sunderland, but I wonder if Vic still speaks German now? 'Noooooo!' he laughs. 'I'm useless at languages. I spent two and a half years in Mexico and picked up a bit of Spanish, but I can't remember a word now. My mum taught people how to speak Russian and German and so I asked her, "Why don't you teach me?" but she insisted, "No you're English, speak English." The thing was because I lived in South Derbyshire the slang was so bad it can make even north-eastern stuff sound simple. I was sent to a private teacher to learn to speak English because I think my mum and dad couldn't understand me. My mum spoke seven languages, but South Derbyshire wasn't one of them!

'People would ask me where I was going and I'd say, "I'm goin' woam." That's how all the lads spoke and we were together all the time. We'd play football or cricket according to the seasons, and the game would go on all day. In the early days I learned a lot because the teams were made of men who had just come out of the pit. It would change with the shifts and they used to kick 10 bells out of you. You learned to protect yourself, so when I was offered an apprenticeship to join Charlton, a 6-foot-4-inch centre-half or centre-forward wouldn't step back just because you were a young kid. That was exactly the same as playing on the 'rec' on Coton Park where I grew up. You looked after yourself and I'd give them as good as I got.'

Fate and football are so often entwined. Having won the FA Cup Sunderland's debut European fixture decreed that The Lads would play in Budapest against Vasas, where Sunderland won 2-0. It meant a first ever meeting for Vic and two of his aunts. 'I remember it well,' Vic recalls. 'In fact, I've got some lovely photographs, and I still see them when I'm travelling. When I'm scouting in Budapest I still go and see the family. The Vasas match was very much like the FA Cup final. As a team we seemed to take things in our stride. There was no fear but a great deal of pleasure. For me, it was an added treat. My dad had pre-warned them because he had been in Hungary some weeks before we went out. He'd met his family for the first time in the best part of 25 to 30 years. They hadn't written to each other or telephoned. My dad was the eldest son. It was a case of, "Times are hard, you better get out and make your own way." [Vic's visit] went fine and it was a lovely occasion. I've never spoken Hungarian and they didn't speak English but we managed to talk a little bit. I always said I'd call again, and a long time later when I was travelling I went back. I knew the address and got to the house. I knocked on the door but there was no answer. I was just thinking I'd come all this way for nothing when a voice went, in Hungarian, "Who is it?" I said, "It's Victor, Louis' son – Lajos' son" and the door was opened. Her son spoke a bit of English and told me they'd thought I was a Jehovah's Witness so they weren't going to answer the door!'

In 2017, as Europe sees swathes of migrants fleeing from war-torn places, people just wanting to find a safe place to peacefully bring up their children, it's illuminating to consider that one of Sunderland's FA Cup heroes is the son of people who had to make a similar move after Second World War.

Born in October 1948 Vic was five when the Hungary of the Magical Magyars became the first overseas team to win at Wembley, the Galloping Major Ferenc Puskás outclassing England to the tune of 6-3. Vic has no childhood recollection of his dad's joy at that result but does have a tale that, given his own destiny, once again brings fate into focus with football: 'My dad came to watch Hungary play at Roker Park in the 1966 World Cup. He acted as an off-the-cuff translator for the team. At work they let him take an oral exam, which he passed with flying colours, so he was getting on.'

By the time of Hungary's 1966 World Cup quarter-final at Sunderland against the USSR, Vic was making his own way in the game having become an apprentice with Charlton Athletic two years earlier: 'I played for the school, the district, Burton and South Derbyshire, Derbyshire, Rawdon Colliery and Granville Colliery. Sometimes I played in the same team as my dad, from when I was about 12. I didn't play regularly but it was good because they were great people. I could play. Let's clarify that and say I could virtually make a ball talk, but when you play on a different stage at a different level you don't do that. You simplify things. Of course, there would be opponents who were going to break my leg but then you'd get these big buggers from the back of our team who would tell them to behave themselves and point out I was only 12! I could run as well, so they couldn't catch me. I used to go training with Gresley Rovers. They tried to get my dad to sign a contract for me, as I was just a boy, but my dad said, "No way."

'I made my debut [for Charlton], I think, against Manchester City at Maine Road as a centre-half. I played centre-half in the first team, centre-forward for the reserves and midfield in the Met League for the youth team. That first game against City I said to Frank Haydock, who was an ex-Manchester United player alongside me at centre-half, "Frank, Johnny Crossan's going too far back. I don't want to go in there and get caught out." He was on the right of defence and I was on the left so he said, "Come here" and we just switched over. About two or three minutes later when Crossan got the ball Frank splattered him. They carted him off on a stretcher and Frank said to me, "There you go, young'un, go and enjoy yourself." I just thought, "Thanks a lot, Frank."'

Crossan had been Sunderland's top scorer in the 1963-64 campaign and captained City to promotion in 1966. That City side on Vic's debut, in the month of his 17th birthday, also included Mike Summerbee, the father of future Sunderland winger Nick. The biggest Sunderland link with Halom's debut though was the man who'd picked him for Charlton – Bob Stokoe.

'When I played for Stokoe at Charlton I went to see him,' says Vic recalling his teenage years. 'I earned £8 a week as an apprentice, £9 for the second year and £10 for the third. Because I was playing for the first team I wanted a professional contract, so I went to see Stokoe and asked, "Is there any chance I can get a pro contract?" He said he'd ask the chairman, and a few days later told me the chairman had said it was OK. I signed a pro contract on £15 a week, but what he didn't tell me was I had to pay income tax and the equivalent of £6.50 a week for my digs, because you paid your own as a professional, so I was worse off financially than I ever was when I was an apprentice.'

Stokoe's fiercely competitive nature is relayed earlier in this book in Lance Hardy's tale of Stokoe and his close friend Joe Harvey on the golf course in the chapter on Stan Anderson.

The teenage Halom was to receive an early taste of Stokoe's will to win too: 'Bob at that time was still fit. He used to play in the five-a-sides or ten-a-sides. At the front of the stadium at the Valley there was an ash car park, with concrete toilet walls at one side and iron bars and a wooden gymnasium on the other. He would think nothing of whacking you. There were a couple of times he whacked me and I reacted by pulling a fist back to hit him only to realise, "Oh shit, it's the gaffer." That's what life was all about in the first team, and you had to be able to cope with that. We were OK. Charlie Wright was the first-team goalkeeper and we were playing reserves against the first team. I was maybe 20 or 30 yards out and I shouted, "Here, Charlie" and chipped him into the top corner. He said, "You little sod" and came running after me. I ran down to the other end of the pitch, jumped over the railing and up the embankment because I knew he'd try to kill me for taking the mickey.

'I had a cartilage out when I was 17, so in order for me to get fit Bob sent me across to Leyton Orient on loan. The manager, Dick Graham, had been coaching at Charlton. He was a big fella, an ex-goalkeeper. At that point I'd been playing centre-half, but at Orient they moved me up to centre-forward, where I started scoring goals. They paid me £35 a week, so when I went back to Stokoe at Charlton I said, "I'm not going to play here for £15 when I can earn £35 over there." So he sold me to Leyton Orient!'

It was only five and a half years later when Stokoe signed Vic for Sunderland. In the intervening period Halom had played for Bobby Robson at Fulham before moving on to partner Malcolm Macdonald at Luton. Was it the case that Stokoe seeking his signature for Sunderland would at least give Vic a boss he knew if he chose to move north for the first time in his career? 'I didn't think of things like that. We didn't have agents or anything. Everton had come in for me. I was a midfield player. Midfield was my best position and there was no doubt about that in my mind. I could get up and down, I could get in the box and I could finish. I was Luton's top goalscorer, I think, that year, and Everton had made a bid for me. It was somewhere in the region of £100,000 and I believe it had been accepted. One of the conditions they wanted was for me not to be cup-tied, and that had been agreed. Luton had come up to Newcastle and beat them so basically they didn't miss me!' he laughs. 'We had some good players, such as Viv Busby [later Denis Smith's assistant at Sunderland] and Jimmy Ryan, the ex-Man United player [the man whose clash with Ritchie Pitt ended the FA Cup final defender's career]. It was a good team, who got promoted the following year.'

Long before that, Vic's time at Kenilworth Road came to a dead end: 'Some bad weather came and I didn't play. That pissed me off no end because the move to Everton wasn't being done and I wasn't playing. I was playing in the reserves and I was the top goalscorer at the club. I was just about to knock the ball in the back of the net during a training game when the coach blew his whistle and said, "Stop." I said, "What are you stopping for?" After a bit of a row he sent me off.'

No matter the story there's always the same glint in Vic's eye – the one opposing centre-halves saw just before he smashed them, perhaps like a victim in *Jaws* a split second before the Great White strikes. 'I had an early bath,' he laughs. That's Halom to a tee: fearlessness and fun rolled into one. No wonder he was such a hero at Sunderland. He could almost have been a character in something like *Thomas the Tank Engine*. Imagine Vic the bulldozer, clearing the path to goal with a cheery grin even for anyone he'd just rolled under the tarmac. Vic would flatten anything in his way and do his real damage by putting the ball in the back of the net.

The FA Cup run was already under way when Vic became the proverbial final piece of the jigsaw – and unlike some strikers we've subsequently seen at Sunderland, one that didn't go to pieces in the box. 'Anyway, Stokoe came in for me,' continues Vic, rescuing me from clichés I can't resist. 'Sunderland were playing at Reading in a fourth-round replay and I went down to watch that game. I agreed to go up to Sunderland before the Thursday deadline.'

Debuting in a league game at Hillsborough, where he would soon score in the semi-final, Vic had seven goals to his name by the week of the final. A fixture backlog meant that on the Monday night before the Wembley showpiece The Lads were in the capital playing a league game at Orient. The Sunderland players' primary task was to not get injured, but that's not how some of Halom's old teammates viewed the occasion.

'Paul Went and Terry Brisley were going to make a sandwich of me,' remembers Vic. 'I'd said to Paul, "If you want something give me a shout and I'll get out of the way." There was a bit of snarling. Little Terry had been an apprentice when I was there and he was coming at me the other way as Paul Went came in from behind. I get cold sweats thinking about it because I was going to get slaughtered. You know it's coming so I had to go straight over the top on Brisley. I nailed him and, as it happens, it was a sign of the times because the referee just blew and gave the foul. I would have got sent off and banned nowadays and, of course, I'd have missed the final.'

Having survived, and Sunderland having taken a point, the players could focus on enjoying the build-up to what would become the greatest FA Cup final fairy tale of all. In the national psyche Second Division Snow White Sunderland overcoming the ugly sister of 'dirty' Leeds was a story even more entrancing than the Matthews final of 20 years earlier (when South Shields-born Stan Mortensen scored a hat-trick yet was overlooked in the naming rights).

Infamously the subject of a gypsy curse in the 1890s which stated Sunderland would never win the FA Cup until a Scotch lass sat on the throne (despite being league champions as frequently as any club at the time), Sunderland failed to win the cup until May 1937. It was the month a 'Scotch lass' became Queen and presented the trophy to Sunderland's Raich Carter. The 'Scotch lass', though Hitchin-born, was the daughter of the Earl of Strathmore, Lord Glamis, and was the mother of the current Queen Elizabeth. She was also the great great grandaughter of George Smith, who had lived at Selsdon Park, where Halom and co. were ensconced by SAFC in the run up to the big day at Wembley.

Maybe touched by the legend, Sunderland's preparation for Wembley was more to do with relaxation than royalty. 'Unfortunately – or fortunately, depending upon which way you look at it – I was sharing a room with Hughesy,' chuckles Vic. 'It was ridiculous. If I was watching the telly he would turn it off or turn it over. I'd spend half the night pressing buttons on the telly. If I got my book out to try to read I'd find he'd ripped the last few pages out and chucked them away. One night at Selsdon Park I couldn't find my book because he'd thrown it off the balcony. We had a ball, honestly, it was great. We went to the sportswriters' dinner and had a few bevvies . . . just the sensible eight or nine.'

Although modern day sports scientists may go into meltdown at the thought of Sunderland's preparation, Stokoe's Stars didn't just win the FA Cup they won the affection of the footballing world and the undying love of everyone who calls themselves a Sunderland supporter, including those still to be born but who will learn the folklore. If the preparation was light-hearted, how were the celebrations? 'There weren't crazy parties because we had a game at Cardiff on the Monday night. Our wives joined us . . .' Vic pauses, struggling for the memory, and concludes, 'I probably ruined it . . .' before dissolving into laughter, but managing to add, 'I scored in that game' in reference to the Cardiff match, where a 1-1 draw meant an escape from relegation for Stokoe's old Newcastle teammate Jimmy Scoular.

Sunderland had yet another game to play 48 hours after that, against already promoted QPR, and in between brought the famous old trophy home to tumultuous scenes the likes of which have never been seen since – anywhere. 'I can remember bits of the route,' says Vic. 'There was a spectacle at this end, at Sunderland, that I never expected. We'd got on an open-topped bus at the Ramside. I can remember people outside the hospital, and I thought it was just excitement, but it was the feeling of the whole town. I remember reports that during the period there was record production on the shipyards and everybody was happy. When we got to Roker Park after seeing all these people it was full. I didn't expect it but we were taught to appreciate the supporters, and I think that's what we did. In modern football I don't think the efforts that people go to to watch football are appreciated.'

The next big anniversary of the Team of '73 will mark half a century since that most famous of days. Back then most fans stood, most players were British, the goalie could pick up back-passes, you could thunder into a tackle, and the offside rule made some sort of sense. It was a very different footballing world. 'You could get away with things in those days,' laments Vic. 'The game's changed now and I find it quite hard to understand modern football. I don't see the advances. I see more negatives, because what is very obvious to me is that modern coaching techniques take away the individual's ability. At Sunderland, we played to the strengths of Billy Hughes and Dennis Tueart. The whole team understood one another and played the game that suited them. A small example would be that, ideally, if you can play a ball 20 yards in front of Billy Hughes he'd get there first and be in on goal. Dennis preferred a ball to his feet and would take people on and go past them. Ian was strong physically and had that great left foot. We knew all that, and it blended. You have to play to those strengths.

'This "keep the ball" business where you start off on the edge of the opposition's 18-yard box and you end up back to your own goalkeeper drives me insane. I don't follow it at all. I don't see many players today that are able to show their full gifts because it is all about possession. I am what I am, [and it's the same with] my dad, who was brought up with the Hungarian mentality, which was "I want to go past you, open up channels and play in behind people", so that they were always looking over their shoulders and trying to watch where you were going to go. The Hungarians didn't want to give the ball away but they always wanted to pass it forwards, not backwards. That for me was one of the key issues and abilities I was given in terms of how I approached football. The other one was work-rate, because I'd broken my leg twice when I was five years old. Consequently, one leg is a little bit longer than the other and my knee is permanently bent, and that took away a lot of the pace. I always believed that if I stayed on the move then the centre-half had to work as hard as me, and he wasn't going to be able to do that. My attitude was: I'll work and the man marking me will have to work his socks off. When he takes a break, because he's not used to it, I'll say, "Thank you very much." I would take defenders where they didn't want to be, either out wide or into deep positions. At Charlton I'd learned from Mick Bailey, who played for England, and at Fulham I'd played with Johnny Haynes, who had captained England, and George Cohen, who had won the World Cup. I learned to always be in a position of advantage. I'd get side on with the centre-half because when I played if you were centre-forward and you couldn't see the centre-half you'd get whacked!'

While he is unimpressed with much of modern football Vic is still closely in widespread touch with the game. Having lived in Bulgaria for many years he has scouted over an area including Bulgaria, Romania, Turkey, Greece, Croatia, Bosnia and the Ukraine. At the time of Roberto De Fanti's ill-fated spell of recruitment at Sunderland I provided Vic with an introduction in the hope of helping both Halom and the club.

'I met up with Roberto De Fanti in Sofia. By that time I had been scouting for Sam [Allardyce] at Bolton and Blackburn. I had recommended players to Sunderland. I saw Costel Pantilimon playing when he was 15 years old and he had everything. I think it was a tournament in the Czech Republic and he was outstanding. I honestly don't think that a lot of the people who are scouting are as good as ex-players at understanding what it takes to be a player. Numbers and stats only tell you so much. You have to show willingness, greed at times, aggression. The whole package needs to be there – the skill levels are taken for granted; it's not that so much, it's everything around a player. How much they put in, what their training is like. If you look at a player it probably takes about 15 minutes to know who can play and who can't. I was always a little bit out of it because you're not making decisions you're just giving information to the people who make the decisions.

'As well as Pantilmon I recommended a young Edin Džeko and Mario Mandžukić to Sunderland. If they'd been bought at the right price early on these were world-class players for next to nothing. Later on in their careers their prices go up, and it upsets me no end when the club still has a policy in selling. What I've still got, and take a lot of pleasure in, is a network of players and managers all across the Eastern bloc who still send me players that they recommend.

'We've been on the go for more years than I can remember. We spent some time in Hungary and Greece, as well as in Bulgaria where I've mainly been. A few years ago I spent a couple of years in Mexico. Remember, I'm Hungarian, I'm like a gypsy.'

Nonetheless, like Len Ashurst, Kevin Ball or Gary Bennett, to name but three, Vic is not from Sunderland or even the north-east but instinctively feels this is home from home. In 2017 he fulfilled a long-held wish to relocate to Wearside: 'I feel very comfortable here and, more importantly, so does my wife Heather. She wasn't part of what we experienced in 1973 but she loves Sunderland. Now is a very special time for us. I still go down to the pub and will sit and tell stories for hours on end over a couple of pints. That's thoroughly enjoyable, and isn't it so nice that somebody has remembered you?

'The supporters have always treated me really well. From day one, when I made my home debut against Middlesbrough, I scored, and I think they were happy. I think they appreciated that I wasn't a poser. I would take you out if you were the opposition. It wouldn't bother me at all, in fact, I'd wipe you out and when I'd done it I would smile.' In the way that players have a goal celebration when they smile, invariably a laugh follows Vic recalling wiping someone out! 'I'd have a great deal of satisfaction because that's what they would do if they got the chance. That's what supporters loved to see, somebody who enjoys the work, gives 100 per cent, always.

'For lots of reasons, mainly family reasons, we felt it was now time to be back in England. You have to do the right thing. The choice was . . . in fact, it was never a choice, it was a foregone conclusion. My home in England is Sunderland.'

10

Stephen Elliott enjoyed some great times at Sunderland, scoring the title-winning goal in the 2004-05 promotion season and going on to win international honours for the Republic of Ireland.

An Irishman on Wearside in the era when the club became nicknamed 'Sund-Ireland', 'Sleeves' rolled up to play for Mick McCarthy, Niall Quinn and Roy Keane.

The second S. Elliott in this edition, like Tony Coton, Darren Holloway and Martin Scott from our line-up, injuries played too big a part in Stephen's time on Wearside.

Nonetheless, his time at the club produced some of the happiest and most important moments of his life and, like his fellow forward Vic Halom, 'Sleeves' may not be from Sunderland but he feels that Sunderland is where he belongs. He isn't the first striker to come from Manchester City and find that Sunderland got under his skin.

STEPHEN ELLIOTT

MEETS GRAEME ANDERSON

For those of you who never saw him play – and it has now been more than a decade since he left the Stadium of Light – Stephen Elliott was a top-quality goalscorer: quick, confident, mobile and with an instinctive eye for goal. He was a key factor in one Sunderland promotion and made a significant contribution to another. And, but for a string of injuries which were to have an increasingly detrimental effect on his later career, he would undoubtedly have reached greater heights in a red and white shirt.

He was also one of the very few players to go through his whole career never being called by a name even closely related to his own: before he came to Sunderland and took on the nickname 'Sleeves', he was known as 'Stuey' at Manchester City!

'When I was in digs in Manchester the landlady used to get my name mixed up all the time and call me "Stuart", and the lads I lived with used to call me "Stuey" to keep her confused,' he grins. 'So I ended up always getting called Stuey, and I remember the situation coming to a head when I played in a young Ireland competition and the headline in the paper the next day was: "Stuart Elliott scores for Ireland!" I had five years of being called that and then at Sunderland, I got "Sleeves" because there was an expression going around in Ireland at the time: "Sleeves up?", which meant: "Are you serious?" and I used to say it a lot.

'I never really thought about it until one day Mick McCarthy started calling me Sleeves, and Kevin Kyle too, and it went from there – it's followed me around at every club since, even in Scotland and Ireland. My whole career, I've never been known as Stephen – even my wife calls me Sleeves! We've got email addresses with Sleeves in it. It's strange but you get used to it, I suppose. I can think of worse things to be called.'

On a sunny afternoon, the two of us are chatting in the dimly lit bar of the Maldron Hotel, which sits conveniently on the apron of the airport in Dublin, the city of Elliott's birth. It is a hotel whose fixtures and fittings he got used to during constant travels with the Irish international sides, from youth teams through to senior level. It was also a regular stopping-off point during his time at Sunderland, where particularly strong Irish connections with the club saw him regularly shuttling across the Irish Sea.

As a child growing up in a traditional Irish family, air travel rarely featured but football certainly did, and one of his very first memories involved Sunderland Football Club.

'I remember the 1992 FA Cup final between Sunderland and Liverpool even though I was only eight years old at the time, and I have to admit I was cheering for the "wrong side!" he tells me. 'I was a Liverpool fan and had posters of them, and players like my all-time hero Robbie Fowler, all over my bedroom wall when I was growing up.'

Elliott's talent for football and for finishing, in particular, emerged early, and after his displays for the Republic of Ireland Under-17s he was snapped up as a prospect in 2003 by Joe Royle, who was in charge of a Manchester City side slowly starting to climb out of the lower divisions. It was under only under Kevin Keegan though, that he was picked out of the youth pool and began to flourish in the first-team squad.

'When I signed for City they were in the third tier, but by the time I arrived they were in the Championship and a year later in the Premier League, so it was a real challenge,' recalls the forward. 'I top-scored, though, for Ireland in the 2003 FIFA World Youth Championships, and that may have helped. Keegan brought me into the first-team squad and I got a couple of first-team appearances from the subs' bench before the end of the season, but it was very hard to break into that team. Up front, they had Nicolas Anelka, my hero Robbie Fowler – and what a finisher he was by the way, best I've ever seen – Paulo Wanchope and also Jon Macken, who was banging them in at the time. So, although I was making progress, I had a big decision to make. I was offered a new contract by City and could have stayed, but I was now 20 and I'd made my mind up I'd wanted to play first-team football.'

Elliott had options when he left but it came down to two clubs: Celtic or Sunderland.

'I went up for the Henrik Larsson testimonial and they treated me very well and then I came back down and saw Sunderland and as soon as that happened my mind was pretty much made up straight away,' recalls Elliott. 'I'd known Mick loosely through the Irish international set-up, but there was a warmness about him and I thought, "Yeah, I want to play for you." I was also really impressed by the Stadium of Light. At the time, it still felt very much a new stadium, and it was fantastic.'

Sunderland were still reeling but recovering from failing to go up in the play-offs the previous season. The scale of the disappointment was brought home to the young striker the first time he visited McCarthy's office at the stadium and noticed a big dent in the wall. The hole had been caused by the manager losing the plot and trashing the room, minutes after his side had lost the play-off semi-final penalty shoot-out – the shoot-out in which midfielder Jeff Whitley famously (or infamously) chipped his shot straight at the keeper.

'I knew Jeff Whitley at Man City, so I could understand why Mick was so annoyed,' smiles Elliott. 'If you're Julio Arca you might be forgiven for trying to dink a penalty in that situation, but not Jeff!

'Anyway, it was all good and I signed. Celtic had offered me a little more financially but I was thinking more of where I might make a name for myself. Besides, I got a really good vibe from Sunderland: everywhere I went, from the hotel to the surrounding areas, everyone was so friendly and it reminded me a lot of Ireland. I instinctively felt I could be happy there.

'I was one of a few young lads he brought in that summer – Dean Whitehead from Oxford United, Liam Lawrence from Mansfield Town, and Mark Lynch from Man United were others. He also brought in Steve Caldwell from Newcastle United, who was a little older and more mature as a player.

'I got on with everyone straight away, including Kevin Kyle – although I think I was one of the few, because Kev had plenty of fallings out with people over the course of time,' he says of the big Sunderland striker. 'My debut in the 2004-05 season was Coventry City away – not my greatest game. Peter Reid was Coventry manager, George McCartney gave away a stupid penalty, and we ended up losing 2-0.

'But the second game was against Crewe and I scored a good goal – a long run from our half – and the crowd warmed to me straight away, probably because I was a bit of an unknown. That goal really settled me, and to have my mam and dad over for the match made it a great feeling. You have to bear in mind I was a young lad who had played a lot of reserve-team football, and this was suddenly the big stage for me – it was by no means certain I would make the grade. I think Mick's plan was to use little and large – Kevin Kyle and Marcus Stewart – as a first-choice partnership, with me an option later in the game.

'But then Kevin, who had been carrying a bad hip injury, was forced out not very far into the season, and I got more and more of a chance.

'It was very sad for Kyler because he was a better player than most people gave him credit for, and I don't think he was ever quite the same player after the hip surgeries he had to go through.

'As for Mick, I don't think he ever wanted to have two midgets playing up front, but it worked really well. I played with a freedom and I was fearless and I think that helped spark Marcus too, because he could feed off my energy and my enthusiasm.'

Kyle's season was over before the end of August, and that gave the young striker the chance of the regular first-team football he craved. Elliott and Stewart were to be involved in more than 40 games each for Sunderland that campaign, the Irishman scoring 16 goals, the Englishman 17. They were the only two Black Cats to make it into double figures.

'I gave it my all,' recalls Elliott. 'I'd scored all the way through my teams, at home, at Man City, for Ireland – it was what I was known for – and I would go for goal every chance I got at Sunderland.

'But I had other attributes. I worked hard. That was driven into me in my Man City days and I never forgot it: if it's not coming off for you, then just keep working hard because no opponent can stop you from working hard. That stood me, and a lot of the other Irish lads at City, in good stead throughout their careers, and that was also something Mick was really strong on. If you weren't going to work hard, you weren't going to be in his team, and I think a few players fell foul of that at Sunderland at times, especially Sean Thornton, who probably would have played a lot more.'

Midfielder Thornton was one of those players that come along periodically in Sunderland's history: bags of talent but never, it seems, enough application to make the most of it.

'When we were kids in the Irish squads, Sean was head and shoulders above everybody else, but I think he would admit he could have made a lot more of himself,' says Elliott. 'It's a case of each to his own, and I'm sure Sean will have his own views, but from my own point of view, I've got no regrets about making the most of my abilities because I really was focused on my football.'

The next few months were a real learning curve for the man-boy forward. On the one hand, he went through a 10-day spell of scoring for club and country – that goal against Crewe followed by notching for the Republic of Ireland Under-21s. On the other, he vividly remembers a tongue-lashing from his manager for persistently laughing on a plane journey back from a 2-1 defeat at Plymouth Argyle.

'The players had taken the game seriously but we were having a laugh on the way back and I got a fit of the giggles, and Mick came storming down demanding to know why we were laughing,' says Elliott. 'He told me we'd just lost a game of football and that getting beaten was no laughing matter. It was a reality check for me – I was no longer just a lad along for the ride any more, as I'd thought. I had to watch how I behaved. Mick was making it clear that players had responsibilities and expectations and I realised now I was a proper first-team player and had to act as such.'

Elliott made some amends with a goal-poacher's strike in a draw against Wigan Athletic the following week as August drew to a close.

And a four-goals-in-four-games burst from the striker helped the club climb into the top six in September on the back of four straight wins.

'It was a great spell. I was playing with freedom and no pressure and Marcus Stewart was a big help to me,' says the Irishman. 'I'd seen him play for Ipswich and he'd scored a lot of goals. He was quite well known so I was using him to learn from, and he was great on the pitch in telling me where to go and where to move and that was great because I had so much to learn about game management. That first season I was playing against defenders I didn't have a clue about, but Marcus often did and he would give me tips and hints. Not that I worried too much about my opponents – back then football was very simple to me: there were defenders, midfielders and forwards, and I was a forward. My job was to score goals.

'It was great to have gone from not playing any first-team football and being on the periphery to playing in front of crazy, passionate fans, scoring goals and hearing them chanting your name. It made you feel proud and I was loving it. After September, we were never really that far away from being in contention for promotion. I remember in November we were fourth (but five points behind Ipswich and six behind Wigan at the top) when we played Ipswich, who had Darren Bent in their side. I scored in a 2-0 win and you could feel we were getting closer.'

It took until the last week of February though to finally break into the top two at the expense of Ipswich, and then Elliott scored against Crewe again in early March, the only goal of the game, as Sunderland strengthened their hold on the automatic promotion places.

That was one of 11 wins in the last 13 matches of the campaign which saw Sunderland go up as champions and win the league by seven points.

For Elliott, that superb run was pretty much one long highlight, with promotion clinched as the Black Cats did the double over Leicester City at the end of April, McCarthy weeping tears of joy and relief on the touchline.

Two other games stand out for the striker, though: the victory over promotion rivals Wigan on 5 April; and the night the title was clinched, away at West Ham on 29 April.

'The Wigan game was amazing,' he smiles. 'We took 7,400 fans down and we ran out to see the entire main stand full of our fans. We were all trying to get our heads around it, and it's no surprise that we won that game: it felt like a home match with the noise our fans made.

'Then a personal highlight for me was the win over West Ham, which gave us the title: a night game, full of atmosphere with our huge and noisy away support. We went a goal down but we were full of confidence and we equalised and then I came on as a substitute and clipped one home from a narrow angle, left foot, in the last minute or two of the game. Sunderland had a big following behind that end and I just went into them. Champions! We were champions! That moment was amazing – the roar and the smiles – and I was on top of the world, scoring the goal that gave us the title. For me it was brilliant: it was a really important goal and the Sky cameras were there – and we were league champions – and it's a great moment to be that player.

'I'm naturally right-footed but, come to think of it, I think all my best goals were scored with my left. Maybe it's because you concentrate that fraction more with your weaker foot?'

It was the happiest and best season of Young Player of the Year Elliott's career, a season in which he also made his first senior appearance for the Republic of Ireland. But he says one of the best things about it all was the togetherness and team spirit.

'I scored goals, and I scored some good goals, so I felt I more than played my part. But it was a team effort and we were a young side all pulling together. I never played with a left-wing pairing better than George McCartney and Julio Arca, while Liam Lawrence and Dean Whitehead had phenomenal energy and desire. George was brilliant in my first year: he was the best full-back in the league and him and Julio were amazing down that left flank. To have them, as a forward player, being able to rely on their link-up play was fantastic.

'You talk about what I brought to the team that year but you have to remember you are playing with players of that quality full of confidence. The two of them were on a different wavelength to the rest of us in the way they swapped positions, and Julio was one of the most skilful players I ever played with. He was actually that good he was ridiculous, but very much a team player as well. The focus we had among so many players in the team was great, and Mick kept everyone level-headed.

'I loved the open-top bus parade in the city afterwards, going over the Wear Bridge and those celebrations. It brought us and the fans together – it was an amazing time. Those are some of the best memories I have in football, and looking back on your career at the end, you enjoy those moments because it's a way of celebrating the achievement with the fans and sharing it without pressure.

'I'm never going to match that first season at Sunderland. I got promoted again a couple of years later and played my part and I was lucky to win a few trophies in my career too, but that first season where everything clicked into gear at Sunderland was one long, fond memory.'

The feel-good factor was not to last though. Despite the end-of-season confidence, optimism was sapped when it became clear McCarthy was shopping in the pound shop rather than Harrods when it came to transfers to strengthen the squad for the Premier League.

'Nothing was ever said about budgets but you could tell Mick didn't have much money to spend by the names that were coming in,' remembers Elliott. 'No disrespect to any of the players, but what we really needed was some big-name Premier League names with experience, but none of the signings were real names, apart from maybe Jon Stead, who was highly rated, and Alan Stubbs, who never really bought into the club.'

The 2005-06 season was to be a disaster for Sunderland – only 15 points taken from the whole of the campaign – and a huge personal disappointment for Elliott, who was to be overlooked and then injured.

Mick McCarthy brought in Stead, Andy Gray and Anthony Le Tallec on loan from Liverpool, and with that trio regarded as out-and-out strikers, played Elliott primarily on the right wing. The manager's view was that Sunderland weren't strong enough to play 4-4-2 in the Premier League – 4-5-1 would give them more chance of getting something out of games – and that meant one of his leading goalscorers from the previous season playing out wide on the right.

'I was fuming,' admits Elliott. 'Marcus Stewart had gone and I wanted to play up front, but Mick chose to go with Stead and Gray. Everyone liked Jon, and he had bags of ability, but it just wouldn't happen for him, and we all felt for him; Andy wasn't pleasing on the eye, but he was regarded as someone who could do a job physically, and maybe that was why Mick played him.

'They started against Charlton Athletic on our first day of the season at the Stadium of Light, but we got beat 3-1, Darren Bent scoring twice, and afterwards in the dressing room you could sense everyone wondering, "If we can't beat Charlton at home, who can we beat in this league?"'

Sunderland lost their first five games of the campaign, and the writing was on the wall early in terms of the prospect of relegation.

'We didn't get our first league win until seven games in – a 2-0 win over Middlesbrough – and even then I didn't get to enjoy it: I was selected for a random drugs test at the ground and, try as I might, I couldn't pee. It took me two hours before I could give a sample, and by the time I got back to celebrate with the lads, they'd all gone home. I didn't get the chance to celebrate another game that year!'

Elliott, though, felt there was a moment in that desperate season when there was a glimmer of hope for the club. Either side of the Middlesbrough win, there were draws – five points from nine – to lift the club off the bottom at the expense of Everton.

'I felt we were coming to terms with it,' he said. 'After the Boro game we drew against West Ham and I remember because that was a Sky game and I got Sky Man of the Match, with the bottle of champagne presented afterwards to me by Yossi Benayoun. I've still got that empty bottle at home as a memento! I didn't score but I played really well, and I was thinking, "Maybe this is something which isn't quite so difficult. Maybe we've adjusted." For me, getting presented was absolutely fantastic, and the family were there too, but it got even better because afterwards there was an international break and I scored the only goal for Ireland in a World Cup qualifier against Cyprus and, in my opinion, I was flying then. Two weeks after that I scored my first Premier League goal, and it came against Man United, a top United side as well – Rooney, Ronaldo, Van Nistelrooy; they were like rockets – so to score against them was really pleasing. It was a good goal too, a left-foot shot from the right wing, 25 yards out, which flew over Edwin van der Sar and into the far corner.

'I hated Man United – growing up supporting Liverpool, and then joining Man City and spending five more years hating them – so getting that goal was great. But I couldn't really enjoy it because we were two goals down and we were trying to get back in the game. I immediately went to grab the ball from the back of the net but, in the end, they went on to score again and make it 3-1.'

His second Premier League goal was to come in the very next game and be even better, but it was to end in another defeat and even greater heartache, at St James' Park.

The striker sighed: 'We ended up losing 3-2, but I don't know how because we were the better side throughout, but every decision seemed to go their way. We fully understood the importance of the game because everyone was talking about it all week. There was no hiding away from how much this game meant, but I was excited: for me, this was what the hard work of the previous season was all about. It's a great stadium and a great stage, the Tyne-Wear derby. It was a proper hostile atmosphere, even in the warm-up, but this gets you going. I remember it was a crazy game, there seemed to be goals going in left, right and centre, and loads of incidents. They were under the cosh that day, but Shola Ameobi got a couple of goals that came off the side of his head. Liam Lawrence scored a cracker and I scored one of the best goals I've ever scored.

'I had nothing else on my mind but scoring that day, and when a moment came for me, with people screaming for a pass, I just went for it and curled it away into the top corner. It was a fantastic shot, and it needed to be if it was going to beat Shay Given from 25 yards out. The ball came up to me and I took it past Scott Parker, cut inside Jean-Alain Boumsong and then just smashed it. I didn't mean to hit it into the top corner but I just hit it and straight away knew where it was going. It was a great feeling for the goal, and you could hear a pin drop among the home fans, with Sunderland fans going crazy at the top of the stadium.

'They got a fortunate third goal to take the lead, but I always remember the last kick of that game when I thought I'd equalised. Le Tallec put me through and I lobbed Shay. For all the world I thought, "It's a goal!" I turned away, getting ready to raise my hands, and to this day I still think it's going in and I'm going to be away celebrating – but it cracked off the crossbar.

'That summed our season up, really: close but no cigar.

'To lose that game after all the effort we put in was a real bitter pill to swallow. In some respects, it was similar to the Liverpool game early in the campaign at Anfield where we played well – well enough to get a draw – but Xabi Alonso popped up with a great free-kick and that was it. That was the story of our season: we never got hammered but we just lacked that bit of quality needed to get results over the line, and that was all down to the strength of the squad.

'What you have to remember is that I had never started a first-team game at Man City before I came to Sunderland the previous season, I was a reserve. The likes of Dean Whitehead and Liam Lawrence had done brilliantly in the promotion season, but the season before that they'd been playing for Oxford and Mansfield. It was too big a step at that time, and it was always going to be a struggle unless we brought in top-quality players.'

Injuries too were to hamper a squad of no real depth, and Elliott was about to experience the first of the serious injuries that were to derail his time at the club..

'I'd felt my back being sore for a while, even in that Newcastle game, but in the home game against Portsmouth a couple of games later, it was really painful and I was struggling to play,' he recalls. 'That was the game we lost 4-1 and some angry fan came onto the pitch looking to attack Kelvin Davis. I played the following week against Arsenal but I couldn't play properly because of the pain. That more or less killed my season. I struggled to play properly and missed months. It was a stress fracture of the back, very serious, and to this day I have no idea how it came about.

'In my Sunderland career I had two pretty bad ankle injuries and the back injury, and that was very frustrating because the back injury, in particular, came at a time when I was flying, personally. I went from up here to down there, massively, in just a couple of weeks.

'When they scanned it they found I had little fractures in my back – splinters, really – it was very painful and the only cure was complete rest.'

Elliott missed four and a half months of the season.

When he was sidelined, on 5 November, Sunderland had five points; when he returned, 15 games later, on 25 February, they had 10. The first game back in which he started was also McCarthy's last game in charge: the 2-1 defeat at Man City.

'We knew the writing was on the wall and Mick said before the game that if he lost this match, that would be him,' reveals Elliott. 'He started me and Kyle up front, and we actually did all right, but we lost the game because of a Danny Collins slip up in defence, with Georgios Samaras going on to score a couple.

'Kyler scored, again, and we did all right overall, like we did in a bunch of games – just never enough. When you look back at that season, it's clear that the bottom line was that we simply didn't have the quality. We couldn't find the money to bring them in. I think Mick realised that he couldn't do anything about it, and I don't think he was very happy with chairman Bob Murray at the time. But then there was also the fact that some of his signings just didn't come off. Alan Stubbs didn't buy into it, and Mick brought Le Tallec in from Liverpool and played him a lot up front – he was another one who didn't really want to be in the north-east. When he came in, I thought, "Mick's not going to like him" – because he had a tendency to sulk, and he just gave the impression that he felt the game owed him something. He brought in Christian Bassila, who was supposed to be our Vieira – but wasn't.

'And then there was Jon Stead, who we were all desperate to see do well, but it just didn't happen – one goal in 34 games.

'After Mick was sacked he came into the dressing room and I personally went up to thank him because he gave me first-team football and I'm grateful for that to this day.

'I just apologised on my part for being injured.

'He did say to a few of us that he tried his best but his hands were tied, that he didn't have the money to bring in more quality, but we kind of knew that anyway.'

McCarthy's disappearance from the Stadium of Light all but coincided with Elliott's own: he played in Kevin Ball's first game in charge, damaged ankle ligaments and was sidelined for the rest of the season after undergoing an operation.

'A lot of my injuries required surgery and it was frustrating for me because I lost a big part of my career at important stages,' he says. 'I'm not saying we would have stayed up if I'd stayed fit, but that's probably the biggest "what if?" for me. I would have loved to have seen how I might have got on if I'd been fully fit and been able to play my part.'

You might have thought it couldn't get any worse than a 15-point relegation, but very soon after, it did.

Club legend Niall Quinn took over from Bob Murray but was unable to find a manager and took over the reins himself.

Elliott says, 'I wouldn't say Niall was too nice to be a manager but was he was so affable to everyone that people found it hard to knuckle under, and we needed to do that in the wake of what happened the previous season and not having a manager pre-season.'

Sunderland promptly lost the first four games of the 2006-07 season, and when they were beaten by Bury in the League Cup – the team lying 92nd in the Football League – consecutive relegations were being contemplated. A shattered Quinn came into the dressing room after that Bury defeat and promised his shell-shocked players that within a few days he would bring in a 'world-class' manager.

Elliott remembers, 'The mood after the game was really low. I mean, if you can't beat Bury . . . But most of the conversation on the way back was about this new manager and who it could be. We all thought it must be Sam Allardyce, and the discussion was about whether Sam could be considered "world class". We reasoned that maybe Niall was thinking of someone who was world class in comparison to himself!

'But, seriously, in fairness to Quinny, he won his last game in charge, the one against West Brom.

'There was a lot of talk about the "Keane effect", because Roy was in the stands, but it had nothing to do with him. You have to chalk that one up to Niall.'

Elliott can't help but smile when he remembers those crazy first months when Roy Keane came in and Sunderland Football Club was turned upside down: 'Everyone is used to Roy now, if you know what I mean, and he's lost some of the charisma he had when he first took over. But in those early days it was amazing and, of course, it was the exact opposite of the previous season because suddenly quality new signings were queuing up to come in.'

Elliott knew Keane, having played an international game with him when the Manchester United legend was making a comeback in the Republic of Ireland side following his notorious Saipan spat with then international manager Mick McCarthy: 'I remember Roy coming back into the national side and I knew I was going to be playing with him and I just thought, "Fek!" You hear all these stories about him, and I was only 21, but he was great with me. I should have been thinking, "This is great, playing in the same side as Roy Keane", but all I could think of was, "If he passes the ball for god's sake don't lose it!"

'When Roy came in as Sunderland manager I was about the only player he knew personally, so one of the first things he did was to come over and talk to me. We went on a big, long walk around the area of the academy, and he latched onto me and was asking me about the area and so forth. I took a lot of stick from the lads for being Roy's best mate! But he brought a whole new bunch of players in and, like Mick, played me out on the right wing – so, not that much of a best mate!

'I'll never forget that season with Roy though, because everything seemed to be happening at once. We had the Irish consortium taking over, a new chairman, a new manager, this huge media spotlight and a whole new dynamic at the club. It all took off because Roy was able to bring in half a dozen quality signings, and that was all because Roy was Roy. If he rang you, you were coming – Graham Kavanagh won't mind me telling you he idolised him. I was away with Ireland and Kav and Liam Miller were there and they couldn't wait to join. Ross Wallace and Stan Varga had been with him at Celtic, David Connolly with Ireland and Dwight Yorke probably would have come back from Australia only for Roy.

'Once again I ended up on the wing because we had Daryl Murphy and David Connolly, and then Stern John came in. I think I could have scored plenty more if I had been starting up front, but I wasn't complaining because I was getting a game and, at that stage, I was grateful for it. There were good players coming in and I was a bit selfless in that respect, not kicking my toys out of my pram because I wasn't playing in my best position.

'If I look back at "what ifs?", I wonder if I should have been more assertive on my own behalf and pushed to start more up front, but I don't think it would ever have happened, it's not in my nature. I was happy just to be playing for the club and, having been injured so much, I didn't feel I was in a position to make demands, especially when there were good players ahead of me.'

Elliott came on as a substitute in Keane's first game in charge, the win over Derby County, and scored in the following game, the 3-0 away win at Leeds United. But he suffered an ankle injury at Elland Road when he was tackled heavily and missed the next seven weeks of the campaign. His first appearance back in the starting line-up came in mid-November when he scored in a 3-1 win over Colchester at the Stadium of Light, again coming in from the right wing. And his last goal for the club – which came in the very next game, the 1-1 draw against Wolves which brought Keane and Mick McCarthy together for the first time since their World Cup bust-up, an incident that had transfixed the sporting world in 2002 – was one of the most memorable of his career.

'It's easy to forget how big these things were at the time,' says the striker. 'Roy joining Sunderland was huge, and that match at Molineux bringing them together for the first time was huge too. It was like derby coverage in the build-up to the game, discussing what would happen between the two dugouts. I think it was a game both men were desperate to win and probably even more desperate not to lose.

'Wolves scored just before half-time, which was a really bad time for us to concede. It wasn't a great game, we didn't play well, and it looked like we were going to lose, but 10 minutes from time I got a chance and hit the ball quickly and it went in to give us a draw. Roy didn't say anything after the game but I knew he was extra happy with me because I'd scored. You could tell he was relieved not to have lost the game and was a bit grateful to me at the time – but he still kept playing me on the wing, so, not that grateful! I was actually speaking to Mick not long back – he was over with his Ipswich side playing Drogheda in the summer, and I was chatting to him and we were having a laugh about that night. He said he's still never forgiven me for that equaliser!'

Elliott went on a run of games, but the ankle injury he had picked up against Leeds earlier in the season was aggravated in the 4-2 win over Sheffield Wednesday in January and he did not reappear until April after more surgery.

Yet another injury meant that he did not see April out, and he was dressed in his club suit at Kenilworth Road when Sunderland again went up as champions, this time on the back of a 5-0 win in front of massive travelling support.

'Roy was great for making sure he involved injured players, and he took the entire squad down to Luton,' Elliott remembers. 'He knew there was a chance people would leave and, if you look at it, we're all in the pictures, which was a nice touch from him. Roy had had injuries himself and I think he understood the importance of that. He was a good man-manager at the time, and I wouldn't have anything bad to say about him. He came in and did what was asked of him: coming in and revitalising us all and getting promoted after such an awful start. And I think it came at a perfect time for the club because they were in the doldrums after another horrible relegation. I think they needed a character like Roy.

'And after he came in, the Stadium of Light went from a place where you didn't really enjoy playing, because there was pressure and every mistake was highlighted, to one where you did enjoy playing again. Roy came in and took the pressure off the team because everyone was looking at him.

'Looking back I was proud to be part of it because it was a turning point for the club: they went back up and stayed in the top flight for a decade. And if they hadn't gone up that year, maybe the Roy aura would have gone and the club might have struggled and stayed down for many seasons. It was a wonderful time for fans to enjoy and we played some very good football. Jonny Evans was awesome that season on loan from Man United, and he formed a great partnership with Nyron Nosworthy, while Dean Whitehead was a real captain for us.

It was great to see the club being reborn again, but just a shame for me that I couldn't be more involved.

'The stats say I was involved in 27 games, but it didn't feel that way because I came on as a substitute a lot and played on the right wing, whereas in the first promotion I was starting games and playing up front.'

Elliott left Sunderland that summer as the club geared up for the Premier League, but he wasn't forced out by the manager.

'Roy said Wolves had come in with an offer he had accepted, but I didn't have to feel under any pressure to go – the decision was mine,' he says. 'The reality was, though, I hadn't played much the previous season because of injury, and I was aware Roy had been given a lot of money to make an impact in the Premier League. I just felt the club was moving on. He signed Michael Chopra for £5 million, and I looked at that signing and I didn't think Chopra was any better than me but, at the same time, he hadn't had my injuries.

'Roy would not have frozen me out, but he wasn't offering me a new deal either and, at 23, with a young family and needing a bit of certainty, I felt I had to make a decision – and Mick was offering me a three-year deal.

'I'd met my wife Alexa in Sunderland and of my four kids – Bobbie, Joey, Ava, Emme – the first three were born there, so I had massive ties to the area, but I also had to be fair to my family and consider what was the best long-term decision for their futures.

'I made the decision to move to Wolves, and that was the start of me having a million other clubs!'

Elliott went on to play for Wolves, Preston North End, Norwich City, Hearts, Coventry City and Carlisle, and his career continued to be one of footballing highs and injury lows. He helped Norwich to promotion in the 2009-10 season and Hearts to the Scottish Cup in 2011-12. He also suffered many injuries, including potential career-ending medial ligament damage at Coventry City in 2013, which led to him spending 14 months without a club before finally hitting upon the right corrective surgery.

Injuries still beset him, though, and with his father Willie very ill at home, Elliott abandoned the professional game in England, returned to Ireland and took up playing for Drogheda.

Now, the 33-year-old is on the verge of another big decision following the recent death of his father.

'I fell out of love with football because of all those injuries – especially the one at Coventry, and then another at Carlisle just as I was getting going again,' he reflects. 'But I'd love to come back and play a bit more football in England, and I'm also really keen on coaching and have been taking all my badges. So I can let you into a little secret, Graeme, and tell you that at the end of the season in Ireland I plan to leave, come over to Sunderland and maybe settle in the north-east again.

'It feels as much like home as Ireland does, and I'd like to start again.'

Seriously?

'Sleeves up.'

And, finally, as we head towards the daylight and out of the Maldron, I ask him whether, looking back on a career which started so very brightly at Sunderland, does he ever wonder what might have been, but for injuries?

'Maybe for a moment, now and again, but not really,' he grins.

'Listen, I grew up as a Liverpool fan obsessed with Robbie Fowler and got to share a dressing room with him as a teenager. How many starry-eyed football fans can say that? I made my debut coming on for him after he'd popped in his usual couple of goals – and to a young lad like me, it just didn't seem real. In the 88th minute up came the board: "R. Fowler, off; S. Elliott, on." Honestly, after that, everything else in football was a bonus!'

11

Of all the players to represent Sunderland in almost 140 years only six have played more games for the club than **Gordon Armstrong**, and none can match the midfielder's record of an astonishing 59 appearances in a single season. In the face of these achievements Armstrong arguably deserves to hold a bigger place in the Sunderland story than he tends to have.

Although Gordon became the first midfielder since 1973 FA Cup-winning skipper Bobby Kerr to net half a century of league goals, and regardless of his wonderful last-minute header against Chelsea that took Sunderland into the semi-finals in 1992, much of his considerable contribution tends to go under the radar. Now working as a football agent, one of the most consistent Sunderland players of the modern era reflects on a lifetime of being red and white.

GORDON ARMSTRONG

MEETS ROB MASON

Only six of the 1,000-plus men to play for Sunderland top Gordon Armstrong's tally of 416 appearances. Gordon is never one to blow his own trumpet, which might help to explain why his place in SAFC history is underrated, but in all honesty does he feel that perhaps he warrants a bigger place in the Sunderland story than he tends to receive?

'Possibly, yes,' he admits. 'I'm like all players, I had ups and downs. When I first started it was a difficult time in the club's history and there were a couple of relegations off the back of that. Like you say, I'm not one for blowing my own trumpet. I'm not going to say I was this or that, or I wasn't the other. I was just a lucky boy. The way I look at it is I played for the team I supported since I can remember. My dad supported them. I came from Newcastle, so it was a strange one, but it was the team that I loved. When anybody talks to me about it now, what I say to them is, "It's much harder to support Sunderland in Newcastle than it is to come from Sunderland and support Sunderland." There were three kids in my high school who supported Sunderland – me, Martyn McFadden, who went on to edit the club fanzine *A Love Supreme*, and another lad called Keith Atkinson who I still speak to now. We all got battered. None of us had names at school, we just got called "Mackem". That's what we were. We weren't Gordon, Martin and Keith, we were all just "Mackem". I got it wherever I went, with my boys' club as well.

'In answer to your original question: maybe a little bit, yes. It doesn't bother me. I was just happy that I did what I did. I was a lucky boy to be a professional footballer. I loved it. I played for the club that I loved and I wouldn't have changed one minute of it. People go on about money and things but that doesn't bother me either. It's progression. I was luckier than the lads before me: people like Bobby [Kerr] and Jimmy [Montgomery] and all the people I supported as a kid, people like Shaun Elliott and Chris Turner. Wages went up a little bit all the time. It's life, all things change. I know they're super-wealthy now and I can understand people think it's got a bit out of proportion, but I think, "Good luck to them." It's their careers. It's what they've chosen, and they've become stars in their own rights, so whatever your level is that's where you'll end up.'

Gordon is chatting over a cup of tea at the Ramside Hall Hotel in Durham, a regular football haunt. Typically early, he's found a quiet corner away from eavesdroppers and out of the limelight. He's not shy. Never has been. But in a world overpopulated with driven egos Armstrong was always concerned about the name on the front of the shirt – not the back of it. In a team game where so often players are concerned about themselves first and the team second, Gordon was a manager's dream – and a chairman's.

An ultimate professional, Gordon was consistency personified. Rarely would he take the headlines. Even more rarely (a couple of red cards for dissent) would he let the side down.

I'm a slow learner but a learner nonetheless. It took me many years to realise that when people describe a footballer by saying 'he's good . . . on his day' that, in fact, means he's no good. You don't hear the expression 'on his day' in connection with the game's top players. Those at the top of the tree are there because they are consistent. Too often Sunderland's teams have included players who 'on their day' can look brilliant but if they aren't up for the game they can be passengers. Do I need to name them? If you're reading this book you'll know your Sunderland stuff, but I'll start you off: Kenwyne Jones, Stéphane Sessègnon, Jeremain Lens, Wahbi Khazri . . . With each of these players you turned up hoping to see them at their best, in which case they could be superb. They could be match-winners – or losers if they failed to put a shift in.

In contrast, Gordon Armstrong was one of those players where you knew exactly what you'd get. Firstly, for the best part of a decade it would be a shock if his name wasn't on the teamsheet. Almost always it would be, and supporters, manager and teammates knew what he would bring to the table: aerial ability often in a position not associated with being good in the air, energy, commitment, passion and no little ability with a left foot that was capable of producing quality crosses. No one thought Gordon was a world-beater – least of all the man himself – but if you managed to regularly put 11 players on the pitch with his ability and application you'd be counting your league position from the top of the table rather than the bottom.

Tales from the Red and Whites, Volume Two is about picking a team, and Gordon Armstrong was a tremendous team player. One word sums him up: consistency. In the entire history of the club no one equals Armstrong's record of 59 games in one season, a feat Gordon achieved in the 1989-90 promotion campaign.

'I'm proud of the fact that I played the most games in one season ever,' says Gordon. 'I didn't realise it until I read it in one of your books but, once I read it, even if I do something like go on Monty's table and Monty gets up to introduce me, I'll tell him to mention it because I'm proud of it and I think I should be.'

It is a record that is likely to stand for a long time, possibly for ever. 'I don't think there's many going to get near it, and because the way squad systems are, it's unlikely,' interjects

Gordon. If Sunderland did have such a long season again –
there were 10 cup games, three play-off matches and 46 league
fixtures – maybe the only man likely to get near Gordon's
record would be a goalkeeper.

That show of stamina in 1989-90 was far from a one-off. It
was the second successive season where Armstrong turned out
over 50 times, and the fourth of five consecutive years where
he made over 40 appearances. From April 1988 to March 1991
Gordon missed just one of 113 games – being absent for a
game at Oldham on the day of the Hillsborough disaster.

What made Armstrong's achievement even more notable
is that in those 59 games in one season he played all but 20
minutes. 'I remember the game where I came off. It was against
Newcastle. I got so wound up for the game I got cramp. Denis
Smith absolutely slaughtered me for having to come off,' Gordon
recalls. He's not laughing with the passage of time, just reflecting
with a smile. He's not without humour: Gordon's always been a
good laugh, but he's evidently still narked with himself for having
to come off – especially against the Mags, although he did have
the distinction of scoring against them a couple of years later.

Sunderland have had their share of Tyneside-born players
who have retained their black and white loyalties over the years
but Newcastle born Armstrong's loyalties have always been
of the red and white variety. 'It was a strange one,' Gordon
explains. 'My dad was brought up in Hexham and basically he
had a choice. He could either go to Newcastle or Sunderland.
He had lifts to either and he chose Sunderland when he was a
kid. I remember he told me a story about the Man United game
[the 1964 FA Cup quarter-final replay], so he was going in that
sort of era when people like Charlie Hurley and Monty were
among his heroes.'

Playing in that game was another man who was a model of
consistency, George Herd. The Scotland international inside-

forward would be a key man in Gordon's development and, a generation on, still have an influence on Gordon's son James. 'He was brilliant for me,' remembers Gordon. 'Everything he did had a discipline to it. He was a fit lad, even in those days. I don't know what age he was when I started – he'd be in his fifties, I imagine – but he was as fit as a fiddle. You knew your role. You knew what you were expected to do and what you weren't expected to do, and if you didn't do it you were going to get it! He was so enthusiastic, and I was lucky because I had great people such as Ian Hughes who was my coach. He was younger and he took the team. George was above that as Youth Development Officer but he would take training sessions and so would Jim Montgomery.' George was still about when James Armstrong signed for Sunderland RCA in the Northern League: 'He wasn't really still on the coaching side but he was still going to games.

'Ian Hughes was brilliant with me, he really was. He was our youth-team coach and was younger than George, so it was easier to relate to him than some of the older guys. He was all for you being fit, strong and aggressive. I never really properly thanked him for what he did for me. I have done [in passing] but I only see him once in a while. He was a good manager for me.'

Reflecting on his own development, and having seen his much younger brother Chris and son James go into the professional game, provides Gordon with a deep insight into the perils and pitfalls awaiting young lads trying to take their important first steps as professional footballers. It is experience that stands Gordon in good stead in his current day role as an agent.

'I think it certainly helps,' he agrees. 'If you have a really young guy who is about 16 then you know if you have been through everything they are going to experience that's a real help. If it wasn't then there would be something wrong. I always say that once they get to a certain level it's different as it all becomes about contractual things, but in the beginning you should have someone who has a knowledge of football.

'Basically, in the beginning, young people and parents think that football is good all the time and that everything is going to come with it. Football is made up of massive highs and lows. You go through so many different things. You could be flying one minute and be top of the world: you might get picked for England, say, at Under-18 level and think you're the bee's knees; but then you might get an injury and be out for six months. Then you're at the bottom again, and so I do think it's important to have an agent that has an understanding of football, especially in the early years.'

As an agent Gordon isn't swanning around on a yacht in the south of France, making the odd phone call and flying visit for some hardball negotiations with chief executives. 'There's all sorts of bits involved,' he explains. 'The biggest thing, in truth, is to get his contract right. Making sure he's happy with that is a massive part of it, but there are all sorts of personal things that people don't see. There's also a lot of work that goes in before all of this. People just think that you turn up after one phone call and do a deal, but there is so much more. People get involved because they think it's easy money, but I promise you it isn't!

'If you get a lot of good clients you can make a lot of money – there's no two ways about it given the amount of money there is in football. A lot of people think that football agents are thieves who are robbing money out of the game. I'm not saying this is totally wrong but in comparison, for instance, there are estate agents, all sorts of lawyers and so on, who make money out of things. It is how people make a living and, to some extent, it is the same in football, it is just the way football has gone. There needs to be regulation and there is now. For too long there have been rogues involved but I think they've slowly been weeded out now by the agents' associations. It's a lot better than it was 10 or 15 years ago.'

Developing young players is about exactly that: development. Players like George Honeyman and Lynden Gooch have been working their way through the academy system at Sunderland since they were very young lads. Sometimes, talented players such as Richard Ord come through the youth system in one position before finding success in another role. Gordon was such a player whose versatility was notable before he settled down as a midfielder, doing particularly well on the left.

Eight months after his first-team debut he even played half a game in goal against Blackpool reserves at Roker Park. His first-team debut at West Brom in April 1985 saw Armstrong utilised at centre-half alongside Gordon Chisholm: 'It was needs must in the beginning. We were struggling for a centre-half and basically they decided they were going to give me a try. They played me there in a reserve game, I think it was away to Hull, and then we went to West Brom for a first-team game when we were short of players. Squads weren't as big then so I got my chance. I was 17 years old but fit and strong. I got booked after about 10 minutes and Dave Hodgson pleaded my case.'

The Hawthorns' lowest crowd for 20 years, 7,423 in the top flight, saw Gordon's debut, where he marked Albion's top scorer Garry Thompson. Gordon kept Garry off the scoresheet but Johnny Giles' WBA beat Len Ashurst's red and whites 1-0. A month earlier (to the day) Sunderland had also lost 1-0, but in the League Cup final to Norwich City.

Since that Wembley defeat The Lads had been in a downward spiral, dropping firmly into the relegation positions with three defeats. Chris Turner then produced a trio of consecutive clean sheets, but with just one goal scored in that little run the side remained ensconced one off the bottom, only above no hopers

Stoke City who ended up with fewer than half of second bottom Sunderland's 40 points.

Subbed on his debut as Sunderland brought on a striker, Gordon missed the next match, a spirited draw at Manchester United, but came off the bench for his home debut which saw a 4-0 home hammering by Aston Villa. He finished the season by playing the full 90 minutes in the last two matches – at Leicester City, where relegation was mathematically confirmed, and at home to Ipswich Town.

The sacking of Len Ashurst, who had given Gordon his debut, meant that although the team had dropped a division his own prospects weren't enhanced by relegation in the way that Honeyman and Gooch benefited from the drop in 2017. That was because incoming manager Lawrie McMenemy's strategy was to bring in big-name veterans.

It took Armstrong until just before Christmas to get a chance under McMenemy, but when he did, Gordon marked the occasion with his first goal, in a 1-1 draw at home to Crystal Palace. Goals were always part of Gordon's game. In his first year at the club he notched his first goal for the youth team against Sheffield United in November 1983. It was from a corner, as his most famous effort would be almost a decade later.

The strike versus Palace was the first of 61 Gordon got at first-team level, an achievement that made him the first midfielder to top half a century since FA Cup-winning captain Bobby Kerr. At the time of his first appearance under McMenemy, Armstrong was the youth team's top scorer, a tally that included a hat-trick the previous month against Scunthorpe United. He'd also scored a reserve-team hat-trick in pre-season which, when followed up with a brace a couple of days later, saw him used as a sub in first-team friendlies at Hartlepool United and Darlington – but once the real stuff started he had to be patient.

It was another hat-trick that helped give Gordon a big break, but it was a hat-trick from Nick Pickering against Leeds United. England Under-21 international Pickering played just twice more before being sold. It was a move which opened the door for Gordon and once through it he slammed it shut behind him, establishing himself as a regular from that day onwards. He started nine of the last 13 fixtures and the following season played 48 times, all but two of them as starts.

Still a teenager at the end of the season there was a lot of weight on such young shoulders, as a disastrous relegation to the Third Division was experienced. Infamously, McMenemy had done a midnight flit, leaving Bob Stokoe to come in for the closing stages of the season before Denis Smith took over the Roker Park hot-seat.

Under Smith, Sunderland stormed to the title with Gordon again topping 40 appearances – despite breaking his collarbone at Brighton. There was also a first Wembley appearance in the Mercantile Credit League Centenary Tournament, but there would be bigger occasions to come for Gordon beneath the old twin towers in the 1990 play-off final and 1992 FA Cup final.

John Byrne scored in every round in getting Sunderland to the FA Cup final against Liverpool. Goalkeeper Tony Norman's heroics along the way were also crucial, but just as Vic Halom's sensational goal against Manchester City was the standout moment of the 1973 run to Wembley so Gordon's goal against Chelsea was the crowning moment of the 1992 cup run. It is the single moment for which Gordon is best remembered. With the score level in the last minute of a quarter-final replay under the lights at Roker, Sunderland were hanging on. Tony Norman had been forced into a couple of terrific saves but the Londoners had momentum after Dennis Wise's 86th minute equaliser, created by the man who had relegated Sunderland to the Third Division five years earlier, Tony Cascarino. If the

game drifted into extra time it looked like Chelsea would win at
a canter to win a late corner. Then the home side managed to
gain a late corner.

Gordon's header from just beyond the penalty spot was one
Charlie Hurley would have been proud of. The only headed
goal that rivals it for drama in the quarter of a century since
would be goalkeeper Mart Poom's last-minute equaliser at his
old club Derby in 2003. Gordon's golden moment is one he's
been asked about ad infinitum, so I ask him to step back from
the stock answer he must trot out every time that one moment
from 416 games is enquired about. He ponders and responds,
'The one thing I'd say about it is that I'd told Brian Atkinson
to go and take the corner. We hadn't taken a corner like that.
We'd been taking inswingers and I'd actually nearly scored a
couple of goals from them but I told Atky to go and take the
corner and make it bend out. He hit it perfectly and I made sure
I got on the end of it and it flew in. So that was that,' he says
matter of factly about one of the best headers you will ever
see, and in the last minute of an FA Cup quarter-final to boot.
Without it and the subsequent semi-final win over Norwich
City, Sunderland would still be looking at 1973 as the last time
they reached a cup final.

Was it the greatest moment of elation in a long career?
'On a personal level, yes,' says Gordon. 'But the other one was
winning at Newcastle in the play-offs, because that was massive
for me being a local Newcastle lad. Overall I'd say winning at
Newcastle was my biggest moment, but on an individual level
scoring that goal against Chelsea would be the moment.'

As described at the beginning of this chapter, Gordon isn't
just a massive Sunderland supporter, he's a supporter who was
from Newcastle, so beating them at any time meant payback
for all the childhood taunts. Beating them on their own patch

was even better. Beating them in one of the biggest games in north-east derby history made it the sweetest moment of all.

As with their 1974 FA Cup meeting with Nottingham Forest, when a pitch invasion succeeded in getting a game they were losing abandoned, as the Magpies eventually reached Wembley the self-styled Toon Army came onto the pitch and forced the players off as they trailed 2-0 to the G-Force of Gates and Gabbiadini. They reckoned without the C-Force of World Cup referee George Courtney, who told the players the game would be finished that night even if the stadium had to be cleared. After an 18-minute delay on a night of 66 arrests the teams re-emerged to see out the closing stages of Sunderland's greatest result since 1973. As the final whistle blew the players made a beeline for the tunnel as the red and white army squashed in behind the Leazes End goal simultaneously celebrated this night of nights while wondering how they were going to get home in one piece.

This was not an occasion like Hillsborough in 1973 when Bob Stokoe came out to acknowledge the accolades having reached Wembley. It was more like the previous cup final qualification at Stamford Bridge, the month before Gordon's debut. That was a night so affected by trouble that a police horse was in the penalty area when Sunderland scored one of their goals! No one was able to celebrate with the fans that night, and at St James' only one man re-emerged to celebrate with the fans. Of course, that man was Gordon Armstrong.

'I was told not to because of all the stuff that had gone on but it was so special for me and I had to share it with the fans,' beams Gordon. 'It was magic. I'd been in that end. I was there when Gary Rowell got his hat-trick, so they were always the most special games of the year for me. Beating them at their place when they thought they'd won was great. I remember Gibbo [Tyneside journalist John Gibson] as we were coming through the foyer after the 0-0 at Roker Park in the first leg and he was saying to one of their lads, "It's all done." I heard him say that, so to go there and beat them at their own patch was unbelievable.'

The massive highs and lows Gordon speaks about (with regard to working as an agent and helping young players) were never better illustrated than by the high of winning the play-off at Newcastle but losing the final so dismally. 'The Swindon one is a massive regret,' he reflects. 'Looking back it's easy with hindsight but we went away to Majorca for a trip. We should never have done that, and you'd never do it now, but we did. We didn't turn up at all on the day. We'd beaten and drawn with Swindon that year. We thought we were a better team than them, but they were one of the first to come up with midfield rotation where everybody inter-changed, and they absolutely pummelled us – we didn't have a clue what we were doing. That was really disappointing.'

Despite defeat at Wembley Sunderland still went up when Swindon were found guilty of financial misdemeanours that led some to nickname them Swindle Town. Armstrong had heard whispers: 'I remember after the play-off game at St James' we went into the bar at Newcastle and their midfielder Kevin Dillon, who was a Sunderland lad, said, "McKeag's already told us you're up. There's no way Swindon will be able to go up." We didn't know that was right and it didn't affect us at all. Gordon McKeag was chairman of the Football League at the time, or something like that.' Newcastle chairman Gordon McKeag was indeed well connected in the corridors of football power, at one point being President of the Football League, a director of the league and also the FA, where he also served as Chairman of the FA Challenge Cup Committee.

Although Gordon Armstrong is one of several Sunderland players with stories of hearing rumours about Swindon's potential demise, he does not use those rumours as an excuse for the poor performance in the final, where the scoreline of 1-0 would have been much worse if not for the excellent goalkeeping of Tony Norman. 'We didn't let that affect us at all, we just played terrible on the day, and they totally murdered us,' he concedes.

If Sunderland were lucky to be promoted they were unlucky to be relegated after a year back in the top flight. One of half a dozen league goals Armstrong netted that season was a header at Anfield: 'My dad was in that end so I ran behind the goal to celebrate. It was a great moment.' Just over a year later Gordon was in action against Liverpool again, but this time in the FA Cup final. His quarter-final winner against Chelsea was one of 11 goals he scored that season, making him Sunderland's joint top-scorer, but the final brought a 2-0 loss.

'I think there's some pride that we got there, because at the end of the day we were what is now called a Championship club when we got to the FA Cup final. Overall, though, it was a massive disappointment,' reveals Armstrong, who admits, 'I've never ever watched the match through. I've watched bits and bobs here and there but never the whole game. My overall memory is that we didn't play too bad in the first half but in the second they took over with an early goal.'

Although wearing number nine Gordon operated on the left of midfield in the final, with Paul Bracewell and Brian Atkinson inside and David Rush on the right. Armstrong was never a winger, as such, but was very effective in his role on the left of midfield. 'It was a different time then,' he explains. 'A lot of football was played in the air and I was really good in the air. What we tended to do was to knock it long down my side and I'd try to win headers to try to get it in to the forwards. I was never lightning quick so I'd never run past anybody as such, but people knew if I did get it wide and I got time on the ball I had a good left foot and I'd put in crosses, so I'd create chances.

Forwards knew that if I had it the ball was coming in, whereas with some wingers you know it's not coming in because they want to beat everybody and try to score themselves. I enjoyed playing in the middle as well but I played a lot out wide.'

In many respects, Gordon was the model midfielder of the era. He could tackle, pass, run all day, score and be outstanding in the air. Given how consistent he was and how much and how well he played as a teenager it is surprising he wasn't recognised at any international level. This is probably partially because he was part of a struggling team, particularly in his early years: 'I'd got in the shadow squad for the Toulon tournament. That's my only regret. I'd love to have just done something with England even if I was just a young age group. Loads of lads who didn't make it did actually do that.'

Gordon's younger brother Chris won international honours both for England at Under-20 level and later for Scotland at 'B' level, qualifying through his grandmother, so perhaps Gordon might have trodden the same path as English born Don Hutchison, Phil Bardsley and Donald Love for instance? 'I did think about it afterwards,' he accepts.

There was one representative honour for Gordon. It was an occasion where, along with Marco Gabbiadini and Gary Bennett, he played for a Football League XI against the Northern League in the latter's centenary match at Blyth. It gave Gordon the chance to play alongside England legend Bryan Robson: 'I'd played against him a few times, although he was coming to the end of his career, but to play alongside him was great. He was my hero. I just thought he was everything as a footballer. If you want to see someone who is typically English and played as I think the game should be played, it was him. He never whinged about tackles, he just got on with it. He was strong, he scored goals, he made goals, he defended, he'd get his head kicked off – and, anyway, he was from around here as well. The only downside was he supported Newcastle, but other than that as far as I can see he was as good a player as you're ever going to see. It was nice to be involved on that occasion, and it was a good day.'

Robson managed as well as played for the Football League on that occasion. At Sunderland Gordon had signed during the reign of Alan Durban, debuted under Len Ashurst and also played under Lawrie McMenemy, Bob Stokoe, Denis Smith, Malcolm Crosby, Terry Butcher, Mick Buxton and Peter Reid, as well as later playing for former Sunderland man Stan Ternent at both Bury and Burnley: 'Denis Smith and Stan Ternent were the best, by a mile, really. I had some bad ones, but Denis Smith was right up there. I played my best football and I enjoyed playing under Denis the most. They were great years.'

During Smith's best times he and his assistant Viv Busby bounced off each other as Sunderland played good football and gained two promotions in three seasons. 'They were on the training ground together every day. The big thing about both of them was they were both positive people,' says Gordon. 'It wasn't so much what we did tactically but that they were just positive, and when we went out on a Saturday we would want to smash down the door because we wanted to get out there and play for the club and for Denis because we all loved him. He was a great guy. Famously, whenever he played with us, he'd always get his head cut or something, and he would love the fact that he'd been cut. He was still quite fit then, and Viv was just so up for everything, full of life and, like Denis, a great guy. Probably the biggest thing in football – and there's too much rubbish talked about it now – is if you've somebody who believes in you and wants you to do well then, as a footballer, that gives you everything.

'I don't like saying it, but look at Newcastle. Kevin Keegan was never the best coach in the world, but the best time

Newcastle's had in my lifetime was when Keegan was there. Everybody tells me he wasn't the greatest coach but he believed in them, and that for me is the biggest thing.'

While Keegan was an England legend, when Sunderland brought in an England legend in Terry Butcher things turned sour, 'I had a problem with Terry Butcher,' admits Gordon, 'because I'd admired him so much as a player, and when he was with us he was absolutely brilliant: he was class, he was the life and soul of the party, he was positive. And then when he became manager he just completely switched around. He was the most disappointing of the managers I played for because you imagine that, having had such a pedigree and playing at such a high level, he'd understand how to get the best out of people, but he was completely the opposite. Everything was negative, and we weren't as good as such and such.

'You have to change if you go from player to manager at the same club, don't get me wrong, but we'd see it after games. If we got beat he'd sit there for an hour in a corner and not say anything. You can't be like that. You have to get on with everybody. Every football team loses and every football team wins, but you have to be positive and show the boys you're going to lift them rather than it being the other way around.'

Ironically Gordon captained Sunderland under Butcher, despite being told he could leave. The irony was it was Butcher who soon left. There were happier times under Butcher's successor Mick Buxton, albeit ones spent, for a player not used to being injured, struggling to shake off an ankle problem. There was also a newborn son, James, and his own testimonial against Bobby Robson's Porto in July 1994, where the player who was rarely injured could only manage the first 20 minutes of the game – but it remains an occasion Gordon treasures: 'There was a lot of hard work involved. We'd been to Norway and I'd come back early. I wasn't totally fit as I'd tweaked my knee in pre-season. It was great to have a testimonial, and to play a team like Porto was great anyway. They were a good side and there were nearly 10,000 there, which was good for a pre-season game. I was proud to have done it – that was the nice part of it.'

Gordon had played 396 times for Sunderland before his testimonial but would manage a mere 20 appearances after it. After his testimonial cameo Armstrong didn't appear for over three months but had managed 18 games by the time Buxton was replaced by Peter Reid.

Reid's revival didn't feature Gordon, but at the start of Reidy's first full season Gordon came off the bench on the opening day and did so again in the next match. That 1-1 League Cup draw at Preston in August 1995 was just over a decade after his debut but would prove to be Gordon's final first-team outing for the club he had devoted his life to.

Shortly after his last Sunderland match Gordon went on loan to Bristol City. Interestingly the Robins manager was evidently someone who recognised Armstrong's aerial ability – Joe Jordan. Later in the same season, it was Gordon's former teammate Ian Atkins who persuaded him to join Northampton on loan, a winner on his home debut against Cardiff City showing he still had plenty to offer, and the following July Gordon finally cut his ties with Sunderland, leaving just as the Wearsiders were about to embark on their first season in the Premiership.

Southampton, Ipswich, Norwich and Leicester had courted Gordon during his time at Roker, the Saints offering £750,000 in the year of the FA Cup final only for Sunderland to slap a £1m valuation on him, a fee higher than the club's record signing at the time. Many an ambitious player would have sulked at being denied a lucrative move but 'Stretch', as Gordon has long been known, simply took it in his stride: 'Basically, Bob

Murray decided that he didn't want to sell me and I accepted that. There was no problem because I was Sunderland through and through, so it never bothered me. The closest I came to leaving was probably when Southampton were interested. They offered good money at the time but it didn't happen, and there were no issues.'

When the time finally came to leave, his destination was Bury rather than Southampton. 'The biggest shock was going from Sunderland to Bury,' recalls Gordon. 'Bury were in Division One [now the Championship]. They'd just got promoted. It was a massive culture shock because it was a tiny little ground and not a nice ground. I'd say that to the old chairman, and he'd agree with me!'

The culture shock of swapping Roker Park for Gigg Lane wasn't what bothered Gordon. The biggest challenge was coming to terms with no longer being wanted at the club where for so long he had been the most regular name on the teamsheet: 'Definitely, yes, it was hard for a while. I never wanted to leave and I never asked to leave.

'Actually, as it turned out, the move to Bury was a fantastic move for me. I got lucky because it wasn't about the money and I had a choice of four or five clubs, such as Swansea and clubs like that. I chose Bury because I knew a little bit about Stan Ternent. They put together a team that included Paul Butler and also lads like Chris Lucketti and David Johnson, who went on to play for Ipswich. I fell in with a good set of guys at a club where there were no stars. You couldn't be. The whole ground, and where we trained, was all terrible. It was tough and totally different to Sunderland. You had to wash your own kit. Everything was laid on for you at Sunderland but not at Bury. We'd travel to games on the day and straight back, even when we played Portsmouth, but everybody mucked in together and I loved it.

'There was no pressure. At Sunderland if I did something like go to the garage everybody would know me and everybody would want to tell me what they thought, but at Bury nobody knew me and I loved that because I could just be a normal bloke, I could do whatever I wanted. We got promoted to Division One and managed to stay there, so for a club like that, it was amazing.'

Having left Sunderland a season before the Stadium of Light opened, Gordon got to play at the new ground not once but twice with Bury, a Coca-Cola Cup tie preceding a Division One visit. They were occasions that required the lifetime fan to be professional and simply do his best for the club paying his wages: 'That's basically how I saw it. Obviously I always immediately wanted to know how Sunderland had done, but for a year or two I think I did have a little bit of bitterness about having had to leave. I think it's hard not to have that, but it soon went. It was great to go back because I hadn't played at the stadium, so it was tremendous to play there. We lost in the league 2-1 (despite taking the lead) at a time when Sunderland were having a great time. We gave them a game both times, drawing at our place. I should have scored in the last minute but Bally blocked it on the line!'

Gordon was to spend two years with Bury, playing over 70 times before following boss Stan Ternent to Burnley where, often used as a defender, he topped a century of appearances in a five-year spell and captained the club. The 535th and final league appearance of his career came away to Wimbledon in May 2003, his 19th campaign. Still not finished, Gordon made a dozen appearances for Accrington Stanley in their first season after promotion to the Conference, before completing his playing days with Radcliffe Borough and having a stint as assistant manager at Stalybridge Celtic.

It was a long career that lasted almost as long again after his decade-plus at Roker Park. The two male mascots at his testimonial were his younger brother (by 15 years) Chris and son James. Chris went on to make over 250 senior appearances, over a century of them for Sheffield United. Son James still plays for Sunderland Ryhope CA, having been on the books of both Sunderland AFC and Hull City.

So where did the Armstrong family sporting gene come from? 'I don't know,' he admits. 'Both my mam and dad loved sport. My dad played on a Sunday and my mam was a really good runner when she was a kid. My dad's uncle had trials and stuff but there was no big family sporting background. We're all left-footed as well, but no one in the family was left-footed or left-handed before us. My brother was really unlucky because he had to retire because of MS. That was really disappointing because he was a good player. He was far more consistent than me and he had a great career.'

While he still steadfastly refuses to blow his own trumpet Gordon Armstrong undoubtedly also had a great career. His reliability and consistency made him indispensable to so many managers, especially at Sunderland. Only Jim Montgomery, Len Ashurst, Ted Doig, Stan Anderson, Gary Bennett and Bobby Kerr have tales of playing more games for the red and whites than Gordon Armstrong – a man who deserves to be appreciated for his contribution to the club far more than he is generally given credit for.